NO LIMIT
OVER
50

WHAT TO DO WHEN YOU'VE BEEN LET GO,
REPLACED, DISPLACED, OR JUST WANT
SOMETHING DIFFERENT FROM LIFE

BOB POOLE & STEVE DOTTO

DEDICATION

Dedicated to all the generous and caring people who
mentored us over these many years.

BOOMER-FRIENDLY

FONT SIZE

TABLE OF CONTENTS

PREFACE

Is it Time for a Change?

Have you been in the same job, company, or industry for years? It may have been a perfect fit for you when you started, but things have changed—in business, in society, and you. Now you feel it's time for a change, and you want to pursue something different. Does this sound like you? Then this book is for you.

Or maybe you've been replaced, laid off, or even fired. During the beginning of the COVID-19 pandemic, many employees became victims of layoffs when their employers had to pause or shut down their businesses. When they were allowed to begin operating again, many companies took advantage of the pandemic to bring back younger employees instead of the experienced Baby Boomers. According to such sources as Forbes, Bloomberg Law, and the AARP, older workers take a disproportionate brunt of the job losses whenever the economy declines.[1,2] If that's what happened to you, then this book is for you.

---

1 https://www.forbes.com/sites/jackkelly/2020/08/03/companies-in-their-cost-cutting-are-discriminating-against-older-workers/?sh=35010cea4436
2 https://www.aarp.org/work/working-at-50-plus/info-2020/pandemic-unemployment-older-workers.html

Perhaps you're feeling the squeeze. You can detect a change in the climate, and you're concerned you may be forced to leave the job you've had for a long time. If you find yourself in this situation, this book is for you.

Or maybe you're on the cusp of retirement but perhaps not financially or emotionally able to retire. In that case, this book is for you, too.

It's probably been a long time since you looked for a job, and you know things have changed. For example, where do you even find jobs today? If you're a Boomer or Gen Xer (or "Grey Waver") like us (Steve and Bob), you probably remember seeing job listings in newspapers' classified ads section. That is not where you'll find them anymore. You also may not have created or updated your resume in years. In addition, technology has replaced personal connections at many levels of a job search and function. Online interviewing using video apps was common before COVID-19, but now it's standard for initial screening. You may lack the technical expertise to use it.

Then there is the entire world of social media that prospective employers will use to check you out. Will they find you? What might they see when they do a Google search for your name?

Is being an employee—again—the correct path for you? If that's what you're looking for, this book will help you find and get those jobs.

But there are alternatives to devoting all of your efforts to a single employer. These include freelancing, taking on part-time gigs or side hustles, and even starting your own business.

Changing jobs or careers over 50 sounds daunting when you drill down and start lining up all the elements that need to be in place to be successful, but it isn't—if you have a plan and stick to it.

Consider us, for example:

Bob Poole's Story: A few years ago, I was fighting the overwhelming feeling that my productive years were over, that I no longer had the technical chops, and maybe even the talent or toughness, to get where I wanted to go and do what I wanted to do. I often worried about choosing the wrong path, making a bad decision, or following the wrong idea because I didn't have the luxury of all the time in the world that I thought I once had.

When I was in my 50s, my phone always rang with calls from headhunters trying to convince me to join their clients' companies. I have been self-employed for most of my life, offering sales and marketing solutions to clients all over the world. In the 1970s, I was one of the country's top salespeople for my employer, 3M Company. I have always had job offers or client engagements for decades.

However, by the time I hit the big 6–0, those offers had all but dried up. I knew I was the same person. I had even *more* experience and even *more* successes than I had had during previous decades, but no one seemed to want it. It was frustrating and even depressing. Maybe you're having some of these same thoughts. I even thought about the "R" word for a time, but instead of retiring, I rewired! I started concentrating on helping small businesses get online with great websites, design, social media marketing, and sales strategies and implementation. I used the experience I had gained over 40+ years in business to help others achieve their dreams, build their businesses and make a difference in our world.

Steve Dotto's Story: I must admit, retirement wasn't something I thought much about, nor did it hold the appeal that it had for so many of my peers. I've been a serial entrepreneur for my whole life and expected to spend the remainder of it in the same pursuit.

The closest thing I ever had to a traditional "job" was 20 years when I hosted and produced Dotto's Data Café, a TV series that aired in Canada. When it ended, I shifted my focus to the online world, and for the first time in my experience, I struggled.

The online world was so vastly different from the business world I'd been raised in that it took me the better part of five years to crack the code. But once I figured it out, I reveled in the freedom and opportunity the online marketplace represented.

But then I, too, had a rather rude awakening when I started noticing the specter of ageism appearing in my peripheral vision. A few opportunities were closed because the sponsor didn't feel I was "right" for their audience (i.e., I was too old). Even more disturbing was that when I began having conversations with my former colleagues—people I knew to have amazing character and abilities—who also found themselves on the street, the reason was the same. They were being pushed out in favor of younger workers. The shocking thing was that it wasn't always because a younger employee was less expensive. Often it was that Boomers' experience and expertise were seen as "irrelevant." In this online world, memories are short and experience is something that some people think is just a Google search away.

This pissed me off! Seeing the immediate impact of this marginalization on my old comrades, I recognized that we all needed a little encouragement and someone to nudge us in the right direction.

We Boomers and Gen Xers still have a lot to offer! And we want to help others see it as well.

"Nothing freaks you out as much, because you have been there, you have done that, notes Alikhani. I have seen failure. I have seen success. The glory and the misery, they pass. And you come out of it on the other side as long as you persevere."

Nasim Alikhani in How this Former Stay-at-Home Mom Built One of New York's Hottest Restaurants at 59 by Maressa Brown, Dec. 17, 2020, Parents.com[3].

INTRODUCTION

After much introspection and conversations with each other, our spouses, friends, and colleagues, we knew we were right. Even if we'd been pushed aside in our careers, perhaps in favor of a shiny new model, we still had a lot to offer. We wrote this book to show you that there IS hope.

Many employers today want somebody who already has the skills they want and need. Those who have given older employees a chance have discovered several reasons why we're preferable to younger workers. You don't need us to tell you that; there is a definite entitled, whiny streak to *some* younger employees today. This is not an indictment of all young people. But there are some out there whose work ethic is mediocre when compared with that of older employees. They seek and need affirmation and encouragement. They want what they haven't earned and become petulant when more is asked of them.

Employers who have gotten one or two of this type of employee are more than willing to go to the well for older, seasoned, experienced employees.

"You can't Google experience!"

And that, my friend, is what you have in abundance: experience. As Steve likes to say, "You can't Google experience!"

Yes, you may not be up on all the latest technologies. Yes, there may be things you still need to learn. And yes, after you've been in the workforce for a few decades, the temptation to become set in your ways is there, but if you're reading this, then you're open to change. You're looking to move up, to make a change, to better your circumstances. And that means you're willing to learn and to grow. Having been there and done that, we can help you make those changes and add the skills you need to acquire.

Combine your willingness to learn with the things that only years of experience teach. Yes, it can be challenging to look for a job, especially if you haven't been job hunting in years. It isn't unusual for a Baby Boomer to have held the same job for years, even decades, and thus the idea of interviewing and job hunting now is especially daunting. Don't worry! People our age change careers, start businesses, make lateral changes, and completely start over—all the time.

What's more, people who might have been called "senior citizens" not too long ago have made extraordinary contributions to society—many of them late in life.

It's not a question of how old you are; instead, it's a question of how long it takes you to make a difference. Realistically, if you're 65-years old today, you can join a firm and deliver 10, 15, or even 20 years of stellar work. According to the Bureau of Labor Statistics[4], "There is no upper age limit for inclusion in the working-age population."

> "THERE IS NO UPPER AGE LIMIT FOR INCLUSION IN THE WORKING-AGE POPULATION."

If you're in government, the theoretical upper limit is...well, even more limitless. In 2020 we had a presidential election between two men in their *seventies*, while the Chambers of Congress are currently being led by a man in his seventies and a woman in her eighties! Whether you're in the private or public sector, your age is NOT an obstacle—unless you let it be.

Now, it's easy to point to someone else's success but not so easy to replicate that success yourself. You're correct; it isn't easy. It can take hard work. But you're a Baby Boomer; by definition, you're not afraid of hard work. That's one of the incredible qualities you bring to the table and one of the reasons you're destined to succeed.

---

4 Bureau of Labor Statistics, *Technical Notes International Comparisons of Annual Labor Force Statistics, 1970-2012: International Labor Comparisons in the United States.* https://www.bls.gov/ilc/flscomparelf/technical_notes.pdf (last accessed April 11, 2021).

Yes, there are challenges—very real ones—but you CAN surmount them. You need the tools and a plan to do so. We'll tackle those issues one at a time.

Finding Employment, Changing Careers, Implementing a Side Hustle, or Following Your Dream When You're Older

We didn't grow up with the Internet, so it's no surprise that using it doesn't come naturally to us. The pace of change is scary, and our generation is vulnerable. None of us is looking forward to crafting a resume and applying for a new job. No one is eager to face judgment and even rejection from decision-makers who are younger than our children.

But suppose you embrace the process. Wherever there is change or disruption, there is also opportunity. We can find opportunities in that chaos that will lead to the perfect job.

You may think:

"I'm too old."

"I don't have the skills."

"I don't know where to start."

"It's too late."

Have you said any of these things to yourself? Have you found yourself facing a job search, a career change, a financial challenge, or some other massive life change regarding your career? If you're a Baby Boomer like us, you may feel like the deck is stacked against you. Maybe you're worried about age discrimination. Perhaps you think you lack the skills to change your career path, restart it, or *jump*-start it—and you wonder whether you can make early retirement work. Chances are you're not thrilled about the idea (or you wouldn't be reading this). Over 140-million Americans were born between 1946 and 1979/80—Boomers or Gen Xers. Now you find yourself looking for a new job or a side hustle to supplement income or retirement or to start a new career in a completely new field, and you feel like it just might be impossible. Just as businesses during the pandemic needed to reevaluate what they offered consumers or businesses, each of us has had to pivot, too, by reevaluating who we are in the workforce and what we have to offer.

It's Not Impossible

As older people, we often feel passed over. Potential employers may not want us because we're too close to retirement age, don't have the energy of our younger counterparts, or simply aren't up on the latest changes in business culture and technology.

The world of work has changed a lot since we first entered the workforce, and we're not sure if it's still a place where we can set new goals and succeed.

If we're honest with ourselves, we're probably more than a bit frustrated.

When we began our careers, people generally considered 65 to be our retirement age. Now that we're that age, many of us wonder whose bright idea that was! In 1965, the Social Security Administration estimated men's life expectancy after retirement at 75.7 years. (For women, the estimate was 80.9 years[5].)

Today we can expect to spend several *decades* before we shed our mortal coil. Plenty of time to still have an impact; plenty of time to contribute.

Many of us are not in a financial position to retire, and even if we're financially secure, we might not be ready to step out of the game. Work not only defined our careers but may have formed our identities and the basis of our social lives. It made us feel valuable and productive. We were good at what we did. How do we start all over again now?

Our goal with this book is to guide you through the steps that will take you to your next job, whether it's a traditional one working for someone else, one that you've created for yourself as a side hustle, or something in between that provides you with the flexibility to work when you want to work.

---

5 Social Security Online Actuarial Publications: *Cohort Life Expectancy.*
https://www.ssa.gov/oact/TR/2011/lr5a4.html (last accessed April 14, 2021).

CHAPTER ONE

To Find a New Job, You Need a New Resume

We begin with the first fundamental step you must take to find employment: your resume. A resume is the business equivalent of something they say all the time on those cooking shows on television: "Show me *you* on a plate." When cooks create their "signature dishes," they're summing up who they are and what they can do on that plate, right?

A resume used to be the sum total of who you are to a potential employer. Today it's just the starting point. If you're in your 50s or older and suddenly find yourself looking for work, you're dead in the water unless and until you have a modern, up-to-date resume that highlights your skills and accomplishments. And especially if you've been in the working world for many years with no need to search for a job, chances are good you either have no resume or have one that's very out of date.

By "out of date," we don't just mean that you need to add your latest job to your resume and make sure that all the information is current. The resume itself needs to be different. For the most part, resumes are seldom really "read" by people. Instead, they are pre-screened by a computer that uses Artificial Intelligence to scan for critical keywords (typically ones that are cited in a job description). If those keywords are found, the resume will be passed through to the next stage as a match. Therefore, we now write our resume for the computer.

For many modern workers, the concept of a resume or CV is somewhat foreign. For them, the key to evaluating a person is their social media "Profile"—a brief description of who you are and what you have to offer to a potential employer. Browse through LinkedIn, and you'll see the general direction in which we're headed. People's Profiles are their shadow resumes. They inform potential employers of your skillset without directly advertising the fact that you're looking for a new placement.

Classic resumes are still valuable. However, using social media accounts for job applications (and don't worry, we'll get to that) is increasingly important. The fact is that even if employers place less importance on a resume than they used to, every one of them will still ask for it when you apply for a job. (Chances are good they'll then ask you to input all the component information again in their proprietary online systems. Yes, feeding the machine! We'll come to all that, too.) But first, let's talk about the content of the basic resume you should have.

You will find some helpful examples in the **Resource Guide** at the end of the book to help you build your new resume, but for now let's look at the basic format to follow.

1. **Name, address, phone number, and email address.** These should be centered at the top of your resume. Avoid cute or silly email addresses; keep it professional. Also, avoid resume formats that put information into a text box in the document. A text box might look great to you but when that part of your resume is scanned or imported, it may not be imported correctly. You want it to be part of the document so that when it is scanned, the information will appear correctly.

2. The **Summary** explains who you are and what sort of job you want. This makes it easy for people to understand why you think you're a fit for their job and what you have to offer—your skillset. It's okay to have different resume Summaries for different types of employment if you're applying for more than one type.

   Your Summary should also include critical skills for computer-driven keyword searches to find. This is extremely important and needs to be right up front. How do you know which keywords to include? Begin by looking at the job description that you're applying for and identify the keywords that are included. For example, if a job description includes "data analysis," "programming," and "managing" a team, make sure to use those words to describe the functions you have performed. List any programs and applications you are familiar with, such as Microsoft Word, Excel, PowerPoint, or programs unique to your expertise. Include also "soft skills" that are increasingly in demand, such as "communications," "critical thinking," and "team leadership."

And don't overlook company-specific terminology. For example, you may consider yourself a "specialist," but the description uses the word "technician." If that's the case, you will want to go through your resume and change "specialist" to "technician" everywhere it appears. You want to use the verbiage and the terminology in your resume that the people looking for the job have used. If there are any specifics, such as a specific piece of equipment or a particular certification, make sure you articulate this using the same terms and words. This will be really important if you're looking at different geographic regions. If you're applying for something out of your geographic area, there might be a different terminology that they use. And it might be very subtle. But you want to try and catch that. You don't want to assume that the machine is going to recognize the slight difference. You want to make it easy for them.

3. **Work History** should be listed from the most recent job to the oldest. Include details that explain what you were responsible for doing and how you accomplished it. If you are applying for a job where your contribution is measurable, such as in sales, manufacturing piecework, or a range of other jobs, you will want to quantify your accomplishments. This tells employers that you have the skills and experience necessary to do the job they want to fill. In general, describe your previous work experience using "action verbs" such as "negotiated," "achieved," "improved," and so on. (Make sure that you do this in the **Summary**, too,)

4. **Education**, degrees, and more: The longer you've been in the workforce, the more critical your actual work experience and the less anyone will care about your education. It's still important, though, especially if a college degree is necessary for advancement (yes, this is still a requirement in some businesses).

5. **Unique Credentials and Certifications** should be Included alongside your skills list if they're certifications that directly affect, or are necessary for, your profession, such as a CPA license. Other certifications that are "nice to have" but not critical

can appear at the end, such as CPR certification. If you're applying for an office job, that detail would not appear at the beginning of the resume with your skills. If you're applying for an IT job and have particular computer certifications, such as Python, CISCO, Project Management, etc., those certifications will go after the skills list.

6. **References**: Don't be concerned about including references on your resume. If employers want them, they will ask for them.

Once you have a resume, read it over and familiarize yourself with it. Employers will usually talk to you while going over your resume. It won't do to be unfamiliar with what's on it.

By the way, do NOT use a type of resume template found online that suggests you add your photo or uses fancy typefaces and formatting. For some reason, that type of resume is popular or useful, but it looks very unprofessional. If you're using any of the popular online job-posting sites where employers post jobs looking for people just like you, such as Indeed.com, CareerBuilder. com, and so on, your resume will be scanned and sent to prospective employers. Having a photo and non-standard formatting in your resume will make a mess of the scan.

One feature we like on the Indeed.com website is their Career Guide page. It has much good information about writing resumes, cover letters, experience letters, and more. You can find a link and description to it in the **Resource Guide** at the back of the book.

Bob is married to Joann who works for a specialized staffing agency. Over the last twenty years, she has reviewed thousands of resumes. Here are her suggestions:

1. Don't include photos of yourself (or your pets; yes, that happens).

2. Put your education, certifications, and skills at the top of the resume.

3. List work history in bullet format with no long paragraphs.

4. Use the first-person tense when describing your job duties, skills, and so on.

5. Don't worry if your resume is more than two pages long. Some people don't show some of their work experience because they feel that listing something they did years ago will show their age. If it's relevant to the job you're seeking, it's better to include it even if you haven't performed that particular function for many years.

6. As far as I'm concerned, "If it's not on the resume, it didn't happen."

   "IF IT'S NOT ON THE RESUME, IT DIDN'T HAPPEN."

7. Check to make sure dates are accurate and spell-check everything.

8. Make sure your email address and phone number are correct. It's incredible how many times people use an old email address or phone number.

9. List volunteer jobs or additional experience that may be relevant to the type of position.

10. Don't list hobbies unless they somehow relate to the position. For example, if you've worked most of your career in computer support, but you'd love to get a job working with animals, and your hobby is training dogs, then, by all means, list it.

Updating your resume is the first step to moving forward. Once you've gotten over this hurdle, you're ready to tackle what is for many Boomers a genuine issue: lack of technical expertise.

We now live in a world where employers place far more weight on what they find out about you *outside of* your resume. Your resume may open the door, but it will not hold it open for long as your prospective employer starts to do what has become a natural action.

They're going to Google you!

Have you done it yet? Have you ever looked up your name?

> "THEY'RE GOING TO GOOGLE YOU!"

If not, stop reading right now and Google yourself.

This is how you make your honest and accurate first impression. And if you find something in here that's embarrassing or not reflective of your values or ethics, you need to get ahead of it right away. For example, Bob knows someone who, for whatever reason, liked to share stories of her wild dates with men she referred to as "bad boys" and the crazy things she did on vacation. It came back to bite her in the butt when she planned to relocate to a new area for personal reasons. She found it difficult to get a new job but couldn't figure out why until a friend suggested that she examine her online presence.

But don't just use Google to search for yourself. Take a look to see what comes up on other search engines, like Yahoo, Bing, DuckDuckGo, etc. If you occasionally use a nickname, make sure to search on all the ways you could be identified. Don't forget to check Google Images and see if you're tagged in photos on Facebook, too.

You can search your own social networking pages and delete anything you would not want to share with your future boss or Mom. However, if other people have posted about you on their pages and you're not happy with the content, ask them if they will remove the offending post and photo if one is present.

Change your privacy settings from public to private. Take advantage of the different levels of privacy social networks offer.

While you are deleting things, start adding new positive content. Start with great photos of yourself, friends, family, and your pets. Pictures tell a story about you more quickly than anything you post.

You can usually clean up 99% of the stuff out there that you would not want to share. However, if you've been "wild and crazy," you might consider deleting your accounts entirely and setting up new ones.

You typically won't know if something in your social media history caused you to lose the opportunity you sought; you just won't get the job. This may be a particular issue right now due to the divide in the country over the past four years. People's posts and photos have been "tagged" for things they said or did and may define them as someone who wouldn't fit in with a new corporate culture.

Many of you will find nothing but crickets when you search, and while you might breathe a sigh of relief at first, it may not be good news.

Most millennial employers will find it curious that you have been on the planet for six decades when a simple search of your name doesn't result in any hits. What have you been doing? For many millennials, this will be a warning sign. What will they think about someone who doesn't have an online presence?

At our age, there's a good chance that you'll find yourself interviewing and ultimately working for someone much younger than you. Keep yourself up to date with what's happening around you. Use the Internet and read independent news sites. Don't allow yourself to get stuck getting all your news from CNN and the mainstream media. Develop an awareness of what's happening in pop culture. And, if you've been prone to talking about "how things were done back in my day," stop that habit now! Use your experience and offer advice and solutions—not criticism. And while you may not always agree with the younger generations (they won't always agree with you either), you can always be respectful and listen first.

CHAPTER TWO
Become Digitally Literate

A friend of ours told an amusing story about his mother, whom he described as highly set in her ways. She was married to an engineer who ran his own business, and as engineers often do, he was constantly installing "new" technology in the house. Whether it was an intercom system that connected every room of the house to particular other gadgets (including timers for the lights and sprinkler system for their lawn), our friend's mother complained bitterly that her husband was always trying to make things "too complicated" when in fact his goal was the exact opposite. Every gadget or system was installed in the service of efficiency.

Have you felt that way when it comes to modern technology? The first time you read or heard a news story about some new app or social media site you'd never heard of before, you probably felt a pang of regret and even fear. When you don't understand what people are talking about, there's an authentic feeling of being left behind or becoming obsolete. But the good news is that it doesn't have to be that way.

Our friend who told the story about his mother also told me about his *grandmother*. She was a retired teacher who was a fiend for technology. When she retired, she started buying computers (this was when they had first come out). I'm talking about the old Commodore 64 and Vic 20 computers—machines that had tape-recorder inputs and later 5¼-inch floppy disk drives. Our friend spoke fondly of how all his earliest computer (and computer game) experiences came thanks to his grandmother, who bucked the stereotype that older people don't like new technology.

Bob's mother is 93-years old as we write this book. She's been using her desktop, laptop, and iPad to send and receive email, surf the web, play games, and more for almost 20 years. She's nearly deaf, and the computer allows her to stay connected, which is increasingly important for everyone in our online world.

Are You Reluctant to Change?

It's not unusual for people in their 50s and older to resist change and innovation. There are ways to learn just about anything (we'll discuss some of those later in this chapter and in the **Resource Guide** at the back of this book), but you have to be willing to change. You must embrace and train to develop new skills because otherwise, you'll be stuck where you are. The good news is you wouldn't be reading this if you weren't ready to try something new.

You can do it, too. What you'll find, once you start exploring new technology, is that a lot of it is enjoyable. Sure, some of it won't be to your liking. We're not saying that you need to sign up for the latest social media app to make short videos lip-syncing along to pop music or citing the latest memes. You don't need to go back to school to learn hypertext markup language (HTML) or other technical disciplines. We're talking about having basic digital "literacy"—what Wikipedia defines as the "ability to find, evaluate, and compose clear information through writing and other media on various digital platforms"—not learning how to program computers.

Hiller Spires, a professor of Literacy and Technology at North Carolina State University, views digital literacy as having three buckets:

1. Finding and consuming digital content

2. Creating digital content

3. Communicating or sharing it

Modern technology is nothing to fear. More importantly, though, it's essential.

"MODERN TECHNOLOGY IS NOTHING TO FEAR. MORE IMPORTANTLY, THOUGH, IT'S ESSENTIAL."

The "Ways" You Communicate: A Note about Generational Prejudice

We use the word "ways" because there are many ways to communicate. As Boomers and Gen Xers, we've experienced many of them over our lifetimes. Consider this: We're born communicating! As soon as we're born, we cry. We learn how to let others know what we want and what we don't want. We learn many "types" of languages. And to our last breath, we're communicating. That's kind of what we're put on Earth to do. It's the one thing that we do universally. We communicate, and we're so good at it!

What happens is that different generations get caught up thinking that *their* form of communication is the *only* way to communicate. Do you remember being on the phone talking to a girlfriend or buddy? Our folks would say, "You know, they're just across the street." Our parents thought face-to-face was more relevant.

What about the first time you saw family members sitting in the same room texting each other and having a conversation? Bob remembers a millennial married couple sitting in his living room with other people who were having face-to-face conversations. When he asked them why they were texting when they could just talk to each other, they looked at him like he had two heads and gave an embarrassed laugh. The fact is they felt more comfortable texting. They don't particularly like talking on the phone. They get just as much or more satisfaction from having a conversation via text than from "talking." Bob says he felt the same as he might feel if he were having a conversation with a group of people, and suddenly two of them switched to a different language, knowing that he couldn't speak that language.

Whereas in person, we can laugh heartily at a joke or scowl upon hearing unpleasant information, we now convey complex emotional states through punctuation. The written language is evolving. Emoticons (the combination of "emotion" + "icon") and emojis (images, often representing facial expressions but also objects) are now part of our discourse. Videos with no spoken audio track are used to communicate our message across continents and cultures without saying a word. Videos shared on social platforms are quite often played with the audio muted, as they are viewed on mobile devices where the viewer does not want the audio turned on.

We savvy communicators overcome this limitation by adding closed captioning tracks or telling the story graphically. This way, the same video can be delivered into different languages and cultures and still be effective.

If you're reading this book, you're likely over 50 or 60, and you may have your own generational prejudice about how the younger generations communicate. We prefer picking up the phone and talking rather than texting.

You may think of talking to someone on the phone or face to face as the "real way" of communicating. Using instant messaging—a reflection of our speeded-up way of life—to communicate may even be offensive to you. But to a millennial who is the manager of the unit you'd like to work for, it's the only way they're comfortable communicating. And when we bring our generational arrogance to the table, saying, "You know, I prefer a phone call or email or a meeting," then you're going to be looked at as someone difficult to work with.

And speaking of phones, if you're not using a smartphone, don't whip out your flip phone or Blackberry device in a meeting or interview. There might be a bias, and you might be seen as someone resistant to technology. You could also be doing yourself a disservice by not having a smartphone, as it is seen as a necessary tool in today's business world. It doesn't have to be the latest smartphone on the market, but sending and receiving email and text messages on a mobile platform is expected by the younger generations.

So, yes, Boomers and Gen Xers need to adapt and change to communicate with and succeed in finding that new job or that side hustle. If you won't use text or Messenger or Slack or even email and if you don't express capability and understanding in those formats, then it's going to cost you. You need to speak the language of the people you want to convince to hire you.

Steve likes to share the story of his uncle, who fought in World War II. During the war, he became pen pals with the woman he would one day marry.

Jim and Ruby Maxwell

"My uncle dropped out of high school to sign up for the first group of Canadian paratroopers. He wasn't a man of many words. He was a fisherman, he was a hunter, and as you would expect from someone who volunteered to be a paratrooper, he was a man of action. And yet, he wrote letters back and forth with my Aunt Ruby. And they fell in love by mail. They never knew each other before that. And during the war, every letter was censored in Canada. The Bureau of Censorship would take a razor blade to letters. And if he mentioned a pub near where they were bivouacked in the U.K., that whole paragraph would be removed by a razor blade. They knew that every communication they had was being read by somebody else." There were often gaps in delivery, and the letters would sometimes arrive out of order to top it off.

Not exactly the kind of courtship that most of us have gone through. Yet through these letters, this unlikely couple fell in love and developed a bond that lasted for over 60 years.

As human beings, we have this incredible capacity to communicate using the tools we have at our fingertips. And for any generation to think that their communication form is more effective or more relevant than others is the height of generational arrogance.

We have always communicated through gesture, touch, smell, body language, expression, music, and other ways. For us to think that somebody can't be as effective communicating through text is ridiculous. We must adapt. We must recognize that text doesn't have to be our first language. But if we want to be fully participating members of society, we must speak the language.

You'll also need to learn at least the basics of a few programs and apps. Simply put, an "app" (short for application) is a type of software that allows you to perform specific tasks. Applications for desktop or laptop computers are sometimes called desktop applications, while those for mobile devices are called mobile apps. When you open an application, it runs inside the operating system until you close it.

People our age are usually familiar with Microsoft Word as it has been ubiquitous for the past 35 years. Microsoft brought out the Office Suite of Word, Excel, and

PowerPoint. (Most millennials won't know this, but the first release of Office was in 1989 for the Mac.)

You should still have a basic understanding of the apps you will need to transition to a new job and position yourself as technically competent with potential new employers. Think of how this will impress your grandchildren!

Suppose you've decided you'd like to find employment with an existing company. In that case, you need to understand that modern employers want to know that a prospective employee can handle the demands of the contemporary workplace. The odds are remarkably high that the person who'll interview you will be younger than you—often *much* younger—and will have immersed themselves in the latest technology since childhood. In 2018 Bob met a young woman who ran the marketing department of a publicly held company who told him she had just gotten a master's degree in Social Media Marketing—a field that didn't even exist as an educational discipline when we were in college!

We're more connected today than ever before, and modern technology has made remote work and remote learning an integral part of society (especially since the COVID-19 pandemic). Part of dealing with the demands of contemporary work is not looking lost when someone asks you to perform a primary task requiring a computer.

A good friend told us a story about a coworker who was so computer illiterate he didn't even know *how to turn on the computer.* If that describes you, we understand, although it is exceedingly rare these days. The fact is, though, you must have a certain baseline familiarity with computers, using the Internet, and other modern communications tools if you want to be hired. That is because an employer simply does not have time to teach you how to use a mouse, navigate the Internet, or call up and use basic word-processing programs that are necessary to perform almost any office job these days. And while there are plenty of jobs that aren't in offices, in many cases, employees must use a computer to fill out timesheets, check bulletins from HR, put in for vacation and sick time, etc.

Even many blue-collar and trade jobs require some computer familiarity. For example, numerous positions in the construction industry, such as plumber, carpenter, or electrician, require computers to create estimates, drawings, invoices, etc.

COVID-19 Changed Everything

During the COVID-19 pandemic, most employees found themselves working from their homes. This meant they had to use online meeting software like Zoom, Google Teams, and Skype. Meetings and conferences are now virtual. If you can't navigate and be effective in the virtual business world, you'll be frustrated and likely to find yourself unable to contribute the way you'd like. Many online meetings now begin with appeals to "Unmute yourself," "Tilt the screen so we can see more than the top of your head," and "Get rid of that cat filter!" We had a guy from Australia on one of our podcasts who said he'd seen enough cat butts on Zoom calls to last a lifetime. You may even remember seeing the BBC interview with a professor whose conversation was interrupted by his daughter and infant son toddling into view.

This may not be what you want to hear, but do you want to hear the good news about these teleconferencing apps?

They are all basically the same.

All these apps, and countless others, work with your phone's camera and microphone, or a camera and microphone connected or built into your computer or tablet. That's literally all they do. You click on a link (that's sent to you) to take you to a group meeting, or you place a call to a contact from a list of contacts and turn on your camera and microphone. That's literally all there is to it. The locations of the buttons may be different, but all these programs are basically the same, and they're super easy to use once you've tried them. Getting familiar with them is as easy as downloading the app on your phone or computer and then making some test calls to friends or family members. That way, when it comes up at work, you'll know what to do and how to do it.

How to Learn When You're Behind

Getting up to speed on technology is very easy these days. You can learn how to do anything, including how to use the essential tools you'll need to use, by spending some time on YouTube or in a bookstore. There are also online learning portals like Coursera and Udemy. Many of the apps include their own lessons, or you can usually find several more on YouTube. And the good news is that these learning tools are free or affordable.

There are also classes you can take and various on-line resources. Classes for seniors and other older people who want to learn modern technology from the ground up are available through local technical schools, colleges, universities, ongoing education programs, and various other sources. You just have to look around to see what's available, starting with a simple Google search.

Other online resources include YouTube, which is full of video tutorials on just about every subject, and websites devoted to specific topics. Social media includes groups dedicated to topics for learning technology, too.

We would also be remiss if we didn't blow our own horn and suggest that you go to Steve Dotto's site ("DottoTech") as another way of learning quickly how to use the types of apps you will need at work. Go to https://dottotech.com/.

Now, you may be worried about asking for help because you're worried about looking stupid. Don't be. News flash: Technology is changing so rapidly that everyone is behind, and we do mean everyone. The only question is, are you willing to be left behind, or are you willing to learn?

Steve Dotto has spent three decades teaching people how to use technology, but not a day goes by that he doesn't see something new and has to learn something he didn't know. If you tend to get embarrassed by your lack of technical knowledge, apologizing for it, or even being ashamed about it, remember that it's easier to ask for help the first time you see something new than the fourth time it appears.

We're all in the same boat when presented with a new technology, application, or process we don't know. If you take the attitude of "That's cool. I would love to learn that!" instead of "I'm sorry. I don't know that," you'll encourage both your potential employer and yourself.

Sure, you'll have to put up with a certain amount of grief from people who have that "Look at that old person who doesn't know anything" attitude, but you're used to dealing with that already. Remember the first time someone called you "Boomer" as an insult? We do.

The funny thing about using "You're old" or "Boomer" as an insult is that getting old is the goal we're all striving for. (After all, as Maurice Chevalier once quipped, "Old age isn't so bad when you consider the alternative.") Don't let it bother you. When asking for help, simply be direct and honest. Say something like, "I'm relatively new to this because when I entered the workforce, this wasn't available. Can you explain it to me?" Not everyone will be patient, but many more people will be willing to help than you think. Here's the secret: people love feeling smart. If you politely ask them for help and then listen attentively, most of the time, they'll be delighted to help.

Now, will you feel foolish? Will you be frustrated at times? Will it seem difficult? It certainly will. But you're a Boomer. You've faced countless challenges in your life, and you've dealt with them all. You have life experiences that younger people haven't had, and you know how complex the world can be. This is just another challenge and, compared with what you've dealt with, it isn't even a very difficult one. It doesn't have to feel scary. It's just new and unfamiliar.

CHAPTER THREE
Establish a Social Media Presence

This brings us back to social media. It's not enough to know how to use modern communications platforms. You also must be "on" social media and know how to use it because more and more businesses rely on them. We'll address them in this chapter.

The term "social media" is relatively new. Everybody's heard the phrase, of course, but social media is just the name we've given to a specific category of website or application. Back in the early days of the Internet, sites like America Online (which also sold users Internet access through their phones and modems) included chat rooms and other social-interaction sites. Chat programs allowing people to message and talk by text started to become common, as did chat rooms attached to or run by specific websites.

These gave way to "blogs," short for "web logs," and "Internet Forums," which were just elaborate bulletin boards. For a time, chat rooms and bulletin boards dominated the "social interaction" part of the Internet.

Then came the first social media sites, like MySpace, which redefined what it meant to be "friends" with someone. Friends were no longer necessarily people you knew in real life. Now they were people who you met online and with whom you interacted almost exclusively on these sites. MySpace and many other sites like it came and went and were succeeded by other sites so that many people today may not even remember MySpace.

One of the sites that helped kill MySpace but remains popular today is Facebook. There are many, many others – some of them designed for short interactions and some of them designed for more lengthy interactions. We're going to talk about four basic platforms: LinkedIn, Facebook, Instagram, and Twitter. By the time you read this, some or even all of those sites may still be in use or may have been replaced by others. The names don't matter; it's what they do that counts.

A Note About LinkedIn, Business Networking, and Job Applications

If you don't have a LinkedIn account and you're going to be looking for work of any kind, you need to create one. LinkedIn is THE social network site for job seekers and

> "LINKEDIN IS THE SOCIAL NETWORK SITE FOR JOB SEEKERS AND THE BUSINESS WORLD."

the business world. Even people who use it for business may not use it that extensively, but having an account makes you "exist" for many people in the corporate sphere. Don't let it intimidate you; it's just a social media site. And like all social media sites, it has its own "flavor."

LinkedIn is a lot like Facebook but oriented almost exclusively to business. People connected on LinkedIn are usually business contacts rather than friends and family. That's a clue to how it should be used. LinkedIn lets you set up your Profile to mirror your resume. Many employers will ask for your LinkedIn ID as part of their screening process. You can use the site to network with business contacts and find jobs, too. Even if you never use it, you need to have a Profile on LinkedIn in case an employer asks. That profile should be up to date with your latest job information. You want a LinkedIn Profile to reflect your aspirations. And, if your job falls into "knowledge work," you want your Profile to look very professional.

You'll likely be using LinkedIn for job hunting. The site allows you to post recommendations and skill endorsements from your connections (you can solicit these from the friends and connections you're linked to on the site). For this reason, make sure your work history and skills are updated and match your resume. Think of LinkedIn as the place you store and update your professional resume. This isn't difficult; it's just good to be consistent.

And in today's digital world, you need to commit to maintaining your LinkedIn profile. This means keeping it up to date and making sure it's working for you. By posting regularly and responding to questions that people post in your areas of interest, you will have people visiting your profile who are looking for someone with your particular skillset.

"HAVING A ROBUST AND COMPLETE PERSONAL PROFILE ON LINKEDIN IS THE MOST CRUCIAL ONLINE PRESENCE YOU MUST CREATE."

For example, let's say you want to work in marketing. Suppose you post regularly about marketing and have it in your profile. In that case, you will get periodic messages from LinkedIn letting you know about a discussion going on about marketing and inviting you to join in or answer a particular question. When you respond, you will be connected to a whole new set of people who will "check you out."

To get these periodic notifications that may match your skills, you need to have email notifications turned on and check-in and scroll through the site at least once a day when you're in job-hunting mode.

Having a robust and complete personal profile on LinkedIn is the most crucial online presence you must create.

Here are some tips from Boomer LinkedIn expert Joyce Feustal on creating your own LinkedIn profile:

What are the Best Ways to Enhance a LinkedIn Profile?

A common question asked of me is, "What are the best ways to enhance a LinkedIn profile?" Although there are many approaches to take when enhancing a LinkedIn profile, there are some key considerations. Questions to ask yourself include:

When I review a LinkedIn profile, there are three key components I always check to learn more about the person.

* Who do I want to reach and associate with on LinkedIn?
* How do I want to come across on LinkedIn?
* What results do I hope to get from using LinkedIn?

Three Key Components of Your LinkedIn Profile

1. **Your LinkedIn profile photo**. Your profile photo is an important part of your brand and should represent you well. Be sure to use a professional headshot.

2. **Your LinkedIn profile headline.** Include keywords and phrases related to your work to help improve your search engine optimization (SEO). In simple terms, SEO is the process of improving your profile to increase its visibility for relevant searches. Also, reference the types of clients you serve. Add your company tagline to generate more interest in you and your business. You can use up to 220 characters for your headline.

3. **Your LinkedIn "About" section.** Think of the About section as a narrative about you in the context of your current business and past career. If you're a business owner, avoid the common tendency to only talk about your company. Be sure to write from the first-person point of view, which makes you come across as more accessible.

Background Photo, Contact Info, and Featured Section

* **Brand yourself and your company in the background photo at the top of your profile.** Too often, business owners neglect to populate this image. Consider using the name of your company and your company logo and images that show you in action.

- **Make the most of your Contact Info section.** The information in this section is only seen by your LinkedIn connections. Along with your company website, you can reference up to two other websites.

- If you want to include a phone number and don't want to use your personal cell phone number, get a Google Voice Number (see **Resource Guide** to learn how to set one up). Finally, be sure the email address that's displaying is the one you use for your company.

- **Add items to the Featured section.** Feature a LinkedIn post or article that got several likes or comments. Include a link to a landing page on your website, a video on your YouTube channel, or another site. You can also feature a PowerPoint or other presentation. Adding these items gives more visual interest to your profile.

Experience and Volunteer Experience Section

- **Expand the number of characters for the titles of your positions in the experience section.** Each position title can have up to 100 characters. Unlike a resume that typically lists the exact job title, you can add phrases and words that more fully indicate the nature of your work on LinkedIn. As with the profile headline, you can increase your SEO by using these terms. You can also upload a photograph and a PowerPoint or other presentation in your position listing. Plus, you can add links to landing pages on a website or another site.

* **Include volunteer leadership roles as positions in the Experience section.** There are several benefits to adding these roles to this section and listing them in the Volunteer Experience section. First, doing so is excellent PR for the entity for which you were a volunteer leader. Second, you demonstrate that you believe in being involved in your community. Third, people familiar with your contributions as a volunteer leader can write a LinkedIn recommendation for your work with the organization.

Social Proof through Testimonials, Recommendations, and Endorsements

* **Increase your "social proof" by adding testimonials.** Consider adding one or two short testimonials to your About section. You

can also add testimonials to the position description for selected positions in your Experience section. A testimonial can come from someone who's not a LinkedIn connection. Simply ask the person for a quote of about two or three sentences and then modify it a bit, if needed.

- **Be sure to have at least a few recommendations from LinkedIn connections in your profile.** Having people connected with you on LinkedIn attests to the value of working with you. This is powerful social proof.

- **Solicit endorsements for your most important skills in the Skills and Endorsements section.** Send emails to business colleagues, especially clients, referral partners, and others in your field, asking them to endorse these skills. Although not as critical as testimonials and recommendations, these endorsements are still valuable social proof.

In summary, when enhancing your LinkedIn profile, don't forget the basics: your profile photo, headline, and About section. Once those are squared away, start enhancing your profile by applying these recommendations. Doing so will really pay off!

You can find a link to Joyce Feustel's personal LinkedIn profile in the **Resource Guide** at the end of the book.

Facebook: Communicate With Friends, Family, and Strangers. Share Photos, Videos, and Your Viewpoint About Anything!

Facebook is a one-stop social media site. Originally, its
primary purpose was to let family and friends connect
and share photos and, eventually, videos. You can communicate with old and new friends by posting on "your
timeline" or by Instant Messages, join discussion groups
(which you access through a specific area of the site),
trade private messages with people on your "friends list,"
and stay in touch with friends and family. That means
that whenever you post something on Facebook, the people connected to you will see this in the stream of your
posts on a virtual wall called "your timeline."

Facebook is the primary way many family members
stay in touch. You can create private groups, join public
special interest groups, and consume a lot of different
entertainment on Facebook.

Social Media Is Not a Destination; It's a Habit!

Facebook allows you to share all
the details of your life. For example, how you're feeling, where you
are at any moment, what you're

— ❧ —

"Social media is not
a destination;
it's a habit!"

— ❧ —

currently doing, who you're with ("relationship status"), and what you like and don't like about anything! And that's why Facebook is one of the first places employers will go to check you out! They'll go there looking to see what sort of person you are. Are you a "good fit" for their corporate culture? This is the fundamental question they want to answer. We don't need to tell you that if your Facebook profile is full of extreme political beliefs, or "unprofessional" pictures and videos, this might count against you. (Millennials need to remove videos of themselves drinking and getting rowdy or joking about shoplifting, etc.). We all value our freedom of speech, and we feel that our social media accounts are our property, and that's true. But employers almost always take the "path of least resistance." They prefer employees who don't have strong opinions (or who have the "correct" opinions as they see them, depending on who they are).

If you don't want your social media to count against you, make sure it presents a clean, professional, personable image. Avoid anything too controversial, especially anything that would be a "red flag" for employers (like pictures of heavy drinking.). Honestly, this is usually more of a problem for young people than it is for older adults, but you never know.

If you need to "clean up" your account, there are a variety of ways to do so. Facebook offers some utilities that let you globally set "privacy" for old posts or even delete posts in large groups. Their instructions for doing this are constantly changing, so we can't include them here, but the good news is that they offer detailed help and instructions in the settings and support sections of the site.

Remember, as we stated earlier, every prospective employer will search for you, and they will find your social media profiles in that search. What's contained in your Profile becomes your "first impression."

"WHAT'S CONTAINED IN YOUR PROFILE BECOMES YOUR FIRST IMPRESSION."

You wouldn't go to an in-person interview with a stained shirt and messy hair. Don't allow your inattention to your social profile to undermine your opportunities!

Instagram: Short-Form Image/Meme/Video Entertainment

LinkedIn and Facebook are the primary sites to use if you're planning to look for employment, but depending on the type of employment you seek, Instagram may be more appropriate for you. While it is more of a "fun" site devoted to pictures, photography, videos, and memes—humorous pop-culture images that often reference things that have gone "viral" in the news or entertainment—it may be ideal for people in arts fields or other creators for whom pictures tell the story better than words. For example, if you have a side hustle selling ceramics or tamales, or if your work is something that can be seen, appreciated, and understood as examples of your abilities, then photographs of your work may be your best sales tool. Instagram allows you to show off your skills.

It isn't vital that you participate in Instagram or any of the other countless short-form apps, many of which exist to share short video clips or pictures, but it can be fun. Potential employers are not likely to be concerned with your Instagram account, which many people use to show off their hobbies.

Twitter: Microblogging/Political Statements

The final category of social media sites is "microblogging." Blogs, or "web logs," are sites where people post their thoughts on any topic. Sometimes they're like diaries; other times, they're more focused and are more like political commentary. A blog consists of posts typically quite long compared with a microblogging site like Twitter, where people post one, two, or maybe three sentences about what they think. It's used for everything from humor to political declarations to pithy and witty commentary.

Twitter is very popular, as are various competitor sites that are trying to take some of Twitter's huge market share. Often, people get themselves in trouble on sites like these by expressing the "wrong" opinions (and what's "wrong" seems to change day by day). The conversations you have on Twitter should be kept relatively "clean." It's easy to get into arguments on Twitter, and if you engage in a "flame war" with somebody, you might not always see the entirety of it as it can be challenging to follow the complete message thread. Hence, your posts can quickly be taken out of context. It's best to avoid getting into a flame war on any social media site.

Twitter has a 280-character limit (which is double its original length). It allows you to communicate quick thoughts, which is a benefit and a risk because it can be used impulsively. While this is something that adults are less likely than young people to do, the risk remains.

You don't need this site, either, but it can be useful for news, entertainment, and even communications with various businesses. Many businesses now recommend contacting them on Twitter for technical support.

You Need a Social Media Presence

Accept the fact that you are going to be checked out. Steve likes to say, "Your first impression is no longer your tie or haircut. It is the result of an online search on your name."

> "YOUR FIRST IMPRESSION IS NO LONGER YOUR TIE OR HAIRCUT. IT IS THE RESULT OF AN ONLINE SEARCH ON YOUR NAME."

You don't have to belong to many of these sites or even use them very often, but these days it looks unusual (or just like you're out of touch) if you don't have an account on at least Facebook and LinkedIn. Employers like to know that you're connected to the rest of the world (and they like being able to vet you by examining your posts, so keep that in mind).

These days, having a social media presence is the same type of question companies used to ask in the early days of the Internet. Every company, back then, eventually asked itself, "Should we be on the Internet?" These days, you almost don't believe that a company is real if it has no website. Well, the same is true when it comes to employers. If they can find no evidence of your existence on the major social media sites, it will make them just a little suspicious.

Create or Update Your Email Account

We know you're thinking, "Who doesn't have an email address these days?" You might be surprised to know that Bob has a friend who is a retired C-Level executive who had never created a personal account. He had his corporate account (that his admin managed), and when he retired, he didn't see the need for a personal account. That is until he decided he was bored with golf every day and wanted to start volunteering for a couple of non-profits. That's when he learned how to create his Gmail email account which he now uses every day.

If you don't already have an email address, create one through one of the free services, such as Gmail. Go to gmail.com (if that's what you choose; there are others, but this is one of the better ones), where you'll find a link to sign up. Click on it and follow the prompts to enter your name, choose a username (what comes before the @ sign), etc. Choose a professional-sounding username. It could be some version of your actual name, like GAnderson@gmail.com (though with a common name, you'll probably need to add at least a number to the username).

If you don't want to give up a personal email you've had for a long time, you may wish to create a second email address to use for your job search, your resume, etc. Besides Gmail, there are lots of free email service providers that are available. First, search for "free email service providers" and pick one. Then, go to the site and follow the instructions to sign up. You'll probably be asked to provide a phone number. It's best if this is a mobile phone number that can send and receive texts. This way, you'll be able to recover your account if you get locked out or forget your password.

If you're using an AOL, Hotmail, NetZero, Excite, or your ISP (think @verizon.net or @comcast.net) you may want to consider a new account on one of the more current services. We understand that you may have a sentimental attachment to that first email account. While someone's email address may not be a significant factor to a recruiter or hiring manager, these older services can be seen as "vintage" by some. We're not recommending that you "break up" with that first account, only that you consider a second account for your job search. Gmail is dependable and has excellent spam filters that help make sure your mail is delivered.

Once you've created an email account, make sure to check it at least once a day—checking it in the morning *and* evening is better.

And now that you have your email address, you can create accounts on Facebook and LinkedIn by following the instructions both sites give you. Remember, never put anything online that you wouldn't be comfortable saying aloud in a crowded room of strangers.

Add your email address to your resume and be prepared to provide your LinkedIn address to prospective employers. Facebook is a good way to connect with people after the fact; it typically isn't necessary for job applications.

Passwords and How to Stop Losing Information

The two "technical" questions we always hear are:

1. "How can I keep track of my passwords?"

2. "How can I avoid losing information that I want to keep and be able to find it quickly?"

The solutions are password keepers and note-taking apps. A password manager allows you to create and store passwords in a vault that is encrypted. Instead of having to remember dozens or hundreds of passwords, you only need to remember one master password to open your vault. Never again will you write down passwords where other people can find them. And, no more having to find out how to reset your password when you forget it.

We recommend that you consider using a type of password manager like 1Password, LastPass, or Keeper. To ensure that the passwords you use (and each password should be unique and used only on a single site) are secure, consider using "generated passwords" – random, diverse strings of letters, numbers, and symbols that are "generated" by your password manager.

Other apps we find invaluable are note-taking apps like Evernote or Google Keep. (One thing you do not need to worry about is this: While Google is a mammoth corporation, they don't steal phone numbers or sign you up for spam texts.) Steve and Bob both think of Evernote as their "other brain."

Suffice it to say, many other password and note-taking apps are available, and there are bound to be more created. So do some research and try some out before you buy. The bottom line on these types of apps is they will keep you secure and remember things, so you don't have to. They may also save the day by getting you to meetings on time and even preventing you from forgetting critical anniversaries.

Personal Website

Over the last few years, more people have been creating their own personal brand presence online beyond a resume and LinkedIn Profile by creating a personal website. Having a personal website can help you stand out amongst other job seekers as it allows you to showcase your accomplishments. It may also shorten the time it takes to get the type of job you want. However, few people invest the time and (perhaps money) it takes to put their brand online.

As we write this in 2021, it appears that most of the people who are using a personal site are in creative or technology fields. They use the site to show off their individual "chops" in their field. Other people who are using them are highly compensated who believe a branded website will help them stand out from the competition. Having your own site will indeed create added value by letting employers see and understand you much more quickly and personally. Plus, your website works for you 24/7 as search engines look for keywords that describe you, your qualifications, responsibilities, and achievements. If you maintain your website, even if you have a job, you'll find yourself being contacted "out of the blue" by companies that have discovered you online.

Unless you are looking for full-time employment in the creative or technology fields or are highly compensated, creating a personal, branded website may be overkill. Designing, building, and maintaining your personal site isn't as easy as making a resume in Word or Google docs, and unless you have those skills and time, you will have to pay someone to help you. The good news is that there are many people out there who can do this for you. There are even website templates (the **Resource Guide**) that only require you to plug in information or photographs[6].

BASIC GUIDELINES FOR ALL SOCIAL MEDIA

1. Understand what's "public" and what's "private." Always assume that potential employers/customers/partners/the whole world can see what you're posting.

2. Stay in your lane—the middle lane. Do not post controversial content.

3. You cannot win any argument on social media. It's impossible to change anyone's mind, so stay out of the fray.

4. Show off a bit. If you have something of value to share or news that will make people feel good, share it, and create positive energy, which will benefit when others are researching you.

---

6 https://www.wix.com/ and https://www.squarespace.com/ are examples.

CHAPTER FOUR

Get Over Your Reluctance to Network and Ask for Help

Something that poses a significant barrier to many Boomers and Gen Xers is a reluctance to ask for help. We've spent our lives getting the job done on our own, and the thought of asking for help sometimes strikes us as an admission of weakness. Maybe we just don't want to look foolish, revealing that we don't already know the answers. Sometimes we're just not sure WHOM to ask. Whatever the reason, this reluctance to ask for help is a problem that you're going to have to get over to achieve success.

Learn To Network!

They say that "no man is an island," and that's never truer than when looking for a job. That's why building a basic social media presence is so vital to success today. If you'd known, in your 20s, that you'd be looking for a new job in your 50s and 60s, how many things would you have done differently?

Even if you would have done just about everything differently, it's not too late to start. Focus on building your network now with people in your industry (or in the industry you want to join). People are very welcoming of friend requests and requests to network online. Users of social media sites are trending older as younger people move on to different ones. You'll find a very receptive audience of people who would be happy to connect with you if you just start searching.

Steve has one rule of networking: Look for the opportunity to help. If you talk to others, first listen to what they tell you about their situation, company, and life. And then, if it's appropriate, offer encouragement, advice, or something more tangible to start the relationship off on the right foot. These kinds of connections with other humans are invaluable for what they bring into your own life. And by listening and sharing your own story, you'll often find that they'll go out of their way to help you find the connection to your next job.

Search social media sites and the Internet, in general, for forums and groups that focus on your interests. Facebook is a great place to start your search for Groups.

To search for a group on Facebook, from your News Feed (your main page), click Groups in the menu on the left side of the page. Then click Discover to see Suggested for You, Friends Groups, Categories, Popular New You, or More Suggestions. You can always use the general Search Facebook to look for any specific group by adding the word "group" to your search.

For example, let's say you're looking for work teaching people how to repair small engines like lawnmowers. You can connect with like-minded people simply by searching for a term like "small engine repair group." Midway down the first page is a link to a Facebook group called "The Small Engine Repair Group." That would likely be an excellent place to network with other people with the same interests. Similarly, a search for Marketing and Sales groups on Facebook found dozens of choices.

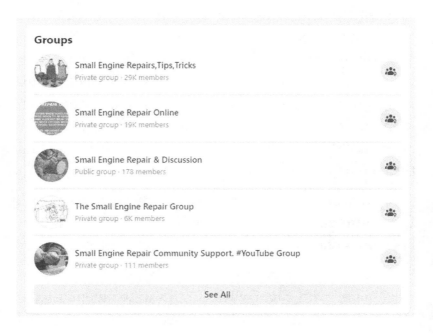

You may have to join some groups and then determine how valuable they may or may not be to what you're trying to learn, but you've got plenty of places to investigate.

Business and Professional Organizations

Here's a perfect opportunity to make use of those professional organizations that you belong to or joined. This is a built-in group of people in your profession who will likely know of jobs in your field.

If you belong to service organizations like Rotary, Kiwanis, Lions, etc., let it be known that you're thinking of making a change in your work situation. Likewise, if you're a veteran, if you don't already belong to one of the vets' organizations, now might be a good time to check them out. There are dozens of fraternal organizations that offer excellent networking opportunities. Don't forget them as well as your church or synagogue.

The chance to network with people who already know, like, and trust you is a sure-fire way to more quickly find and make the change you want and deserve.

Don't Forget to Talk to Friends and Family

As crucial as networking online is, don't forget to do it in person, too. Reach out to friends. Reach out to your family. People LOVE to help other people get jobs. And those connections may be in places you would never expect to find them.

Here's an example. We have a friend who's a technical writer. He once had a bad experience at a job and left after only six months. A year later, he got a fascinating email from the person who got his job after he left! It turns out that she, too, had a similarly bad experience and was encouraged to contact our writer friend by a mutual coworker.

Our writer friend was delighted to learn that it wasn't him but the job itself that was a problem (he'd been wracked with doubt since leaving). But he'd also regularly been getting inquiries from one of the companies where he interviewed but didn't accept a job after leaving his last job. The company he didn't pick still needed a writer, you see, so he referred the woman who'd contacted him. Not only did she get the job, but she held that job for the next decade!

The point is that networking can come from places you might never expect. Would it occur to you to talk to the person who last held a job you got fired from? There are all kinds of ways to reach out to people who are connected in the working world.

Boomers and Gen Xers sometimes fear showing weakness, and they don't want to be made fun of. There's no shame in saying you're looking for work, though.

Find a Job by Looking for a Job

The absolute BEST way to network is to get out there and interview. It doesn't matter if you aren't that excited about that specific job. When you interview, you meet with people who are connected to the broader business world. They may know of other openings at their company or other people in the industry or related industries looking for help. Even if they don't know of a specific job opening, they might be able to refer you to someone who can link you up with someone who does.

Businesspeople know that not everybody is right for a specific job, but they respect anyone willing to put in the effort. If you say, "I may not be your perfect candidate for this job, but I know I can bring my best to any job," you may be surprised by how people react to this honesty.

CHAPTER FIVE

Become Familiar with the Online Job Search Process

A few decades ago, if you were out of work, the first thing you did was find a newspaper and start circling jobs listed in the Classified section. Well, these days, newspapers are almost dead, and almost nobody looks for a job in the Classifieds anymore. That's because companies list jobs online where job seekers are looking for jobs.

Job searching online is the sort of thing that could take up an entire book, but we'll give you the basics here. Remember that there are lots and lots of jobs listed on the Internet, but you have to know where to look, and how you use each of those venues is a little different. Let's run through the basic categories, and we'll explain how you'd use each site to look for work.

Dedicated Job Websites and Apps

There are LOTS of job websites whose specific functions are to let employers post listings so that prospective employees can apply for them. Sites like these allow you to upload your resume so that you can apply to a job listing simply by clicking (and perhaps including a cover letter). This means that, yes, you'll have to upload your resume and details and fill out a profile for each of these sites separately. Sites like these include Indeed, Monster, Glassdoor, CareerBuilder, ZipRecruiter (we've omitted the ".com" after their names), and many, many others. They're geared explicitly toward job seekers and employers. Don't worry about signing up for all of them. Instead, do yourself a favor and do a Google search to determine which sites are most popular right now. You could search for "Most Popular Job-Hunting Sites" and add whatever year it is that you're searching, for example. In 2021 Indeed seems to be one of the most prominent players, while older sites like Monster have fallen out of common use. Glassdoor is another popular one that rose to prominence because it gives users an insight into what it's like to work at the employer's business based on past and current employees' reviews.

Most of these sites let you set up email "alerts" to get regular notices about new jobs that become available. Some have apps that you can add to your phone, too, so that you'll get immediate notifications of new listings.

The AARP in the United States has a website called the **Job Board** where you can connect with employers that value your experience. You can search by geography, job titles, company, and other keywords. Also, you can find both full and part-time jobs. If you're a Veteran, there is a filter for "Veterans Wanted" jobs. If you're not one of the 38 million members already, you can join for $16 per year as we write this. AARP also offers a Resume Advisor tool where you can get a free critique of your resume.

In Canada, CARP—the Job Service for Mature Canadians—has what they call **ThirdQuarter**, an online job service for Canadians (aged 45 and over) who are now in the 'third quarter' of their working careers. Both of these resources can be found in the **Resource Guide**.

At least some job-hunting sites scan resumes and submit them in a way that removes any formatting you may have used in your resumes. One way to counter this is to create a "plain text" resume that you use strictly for uploading. This is a simple text file (TXT) in which the only formatting is capital letters and hard returns. You need to pay close attention to what the particular site(s) you use recommend or require.

LinkedIn and Social Networks

Using social media, including LinkedIn and even Facebook, is one way to find a job. Not only do employers list job openings on these sites, but you may be able to network with people in your industry through them (which means that if you find yourself out of work, you might be able to generate some prospects simply by posting your resume to your network of connections and letting them know what you're looking for). Remember, though, that social media is double-edged. It can help you network, but if your posts are public, your current employer can also see them. If you're unemployed, then public posts may generate some leads.

Also, groups within Facebook can be an excellent place to network. Pretty much every occupation is represented by a group on Facebook. Many of them are private, and you must "apply" to be invited to join. Some allow job posts, and others forbid it, so you will need to check out the various groups. There are also smaller but specific social media like neighborhood websites. Many of these are private Facebook Groups. You only need to click on Groups and then Search Groups. Type in the occupation or type of group you're interested in, and you'll most likely see several that you can check out. You may be amazed at the number of like-minded individuals you will find.

For example, let's say you're a job seeker in Seattle. Typing in the term "job hunting Seattle" in Facebook's search bar (as of this writing) produces jobs in Seattle, Washington, by title along with a button that says "see all" so you can scroll through them. There's also a listing of groups with a button that says, "See all groups for 'job hunting Seattle.'" If you click on that, you'll see a variety of groups that you can scroll through. Some are irrelevant (this search produced several groups devoted to hunting, of all things), but some include "Seattle Jobs & Internships"—a networking group with over 3,000 members. Another is "Jobs / Employment / Work Available Washington State," a group with more than 2,000 members.

Search through the groups, find the one that most accurately fits you, and then join it. There will be group rules you should read and follow. In many cases, you can just post, introduce yourself, and tell the group what you're looking for. People LOVE to help other people find jobs. They get great satisfaction from it. You'll be surprised by how eager people are to help you out.

When You Apply through an Employer's Site

When you click on most job listings, you'll typically be forwarded to the employer's website. (Yes, this means that when you're job searching, you'll end up creating accounts at many, many websites—most of which you'll never visit again.) They'll show you the listing, and you'll click on a link to apply for the job. Then you'll be asked to upload your resume—but the fun doesn't stop there.

After you upload your resume, usually as a text file, a Word document, or a PDF file, you'll be asked to fill out work history and a variety of other information that will strike you as a waste of time. That's because you'll be repeating what's on your resume. It's essential, though, because you'll be entering information in the employer's database that they'll use to screen applicants. Tedious as it is to keep repeating this stuff, you'll get the best results if you fill it out carefully each time.

Always remember that a lot of resume screening happens automatically. Advanced algorithms screen resumes looking for keywords and fields that the employer has decided are relevant or irrelevant. That's because employers get many more resumes than they can realistically go through by hand, so they screen them to eliminate ones that are a waste of time. As we discussed in Chapter One, you want to make sure you add the keywords that match the job description. We've also included a **Keyword Resume** sample following the **Resource Guide** in the back of the book. Your goal is to make sure your resume gets you flagged as being worth their consideration.

Always include a cover letter, too, even if it's just a simple one that explains why you're applying and why you're well suited for the job. There was a time when employers placed a high value on elaborate cover letters called "impact letters," but that's usually not the case these days unless you're applying for a high-powered executive position.

Here's an important tip about your cover letter. Employers are looking for employees with superior work ethics and values. Your cover letter provides an opportunity to mention those traits in some detail by stressing the skills you have that validate your ethics and values.

Words like "integrity," "responsibility," "reliability," "productivity," "problem-solving skills," and other valued work ethics should be part of your letter.

The basic format of the cover letter is to introduce yourself and then explain why you're a good fit for the job. "Dear [Human Resources Manager]" (although you should make an effort to find out this person's name, either by checking the company website or calling the department), "I am a skilled (or experienced) [position title] looking for work in [your field]. I believe I am an excellent fit for the position you've described [then you list the reasons why]. I would welcome the opportunity to discuss the position with you in person. Kind regards, [your name]." It doesn't have to be precisely that; it's just the fundamental way a cover letter is structured.

Once you've applied, it's likely that you won't hear from that company unless they want to interview you. Some companies send out emails that are electronic form rejection letters, but most of the time, you won't hear back. If you choose to follow up on a job you've applied to, that's fine, but be polite and don't contact the employer too often. People are much less receptive to follow-ups than they once were, and the days of "pounding the pavement" to apply for jobs in person are pretty much gone forever.

If you do get an interview, be sure to send a thank you by email right away. It's not unheard of to send a thank you by email. However, Bob believes that sending a handwritten note by snail mail is still the best action. It will set you apart from everyone else who is applying or being considered for the same job. And you want to stand out. This is no time to be a shrinking violet. Buy some quality stationery and envelopes for these and add a personal touch.

Craigslist

The network of Craigslist websites is linked to various cities. Most likely, there's a Craigslist site for the nearest large city where you live. Craigslist is an online classified site that anyone can post to (usually for free). Each city's site has sections for buying and selling used merchandise, social discussions, real estate and apartment rentals, and yes, job hunting.

The thing about Craigslist, though, is that it's much less controlled than a dedicated job website. Its postings are free, and no one qualifies what is listed. If you see a listing for a job you're interested in, you'll usually apply by replying to a "blind" email. That means that until the employer responds, it is unlikely you will know the name of the company posting the job. Because of that fact, we recommend that you do NOT send your resume (which has personal information on it) until you get a reply email that comes from a "real" employer.

Let us stress this because it's so important. There are a LOT of scams online. There are many fraudulent job listings, listings whose only purpose is to get your personal information so they can then somehow get money out of you, search for your private data online, or any number of other unsavory reasons. Your resume contains vital personal information. Never email it to someone sight unseen. Craigslist, because it's an anonymous classified section, is particularly risky for this. If it sounds too good to be true, it probably is, and you'd be wise to avoid it.

That doesn't mean you shouldn't use it, though. Craigslist is one good way to look for local jobs, especially, but as always, use caution. Just as anyone could put an ad in the Classifieds, anyone can post on Craigslist, and it costs less to do so than it ever did to advertise in the newspaper. When you see a job you're interested in, reply with a message saying you are interested and that you have the right skills, but you'd like to talk with someone at the company (and know you're talking to a legitimate representative of that firm) before you submit any personal information. Genuine employers will understand this.

Search Engines

Just searching for jobs on Google or through other search engines may help. Search for the type of job, or specific job title, and the local area where you're searching. A lot of the listings you'll find may be outdated, but some will still be valid. You may also find sites where employers are looking for help and have posted about this. If you do a general search for the type of job or job title, you'll get lots of hits. You will probably have to drill down by geogra-

phy. At that point, you will find that companies post their own jobs on their websites. For example, while Bob's wife uses sites like Indeed and Career Builder, her company also maintains a list of jobs on their website since they are a staffing agency and hire constantly.

Paid Listing Sites

If you don't mind spending a little money, there are sites where you can pay a membership fee and then gain access to special listings. These include sites like **Flexjobs.com**, which has listings for remote work, work from home, and other freelance employment. These jobs are highly in demand, so it isn't unusual to have to pay to access these listings. The site works like any other job site, but of course, you have to pay for access to it. If you don't pay, you can't see the listings.

Job Listings from Your Professional Association

If you have a professional degree or certification, you probably belong to some professional organizations. These may be college alumni sites, trade associations (such as the American Electronics Association or Interior Design Society), professional associations (such as those for accountants, fitness trainers, or journalists), and what's known as "affinity" associations (for the legal, healthcare, and other industries). Regardless of the industry in which you spent your career, there are likely to be groups or affiliations of people with similar backgrounds. Joining or attending meetings of these groups is a great way to find other professionals with whom to network as we will discuss in the next chapter. Many also have their own job boards that are accessible by their members.

CHAPTER SIX

Freelancing, Your Own Gig, and International Working and Living

Freelancing

If you're like us, it's not difficult to remember applying for that first "real job." Bob was 16 years old and found out a local department store was looking for part-time help selling cameras. The camera department was small and was in the jewelry department. He'd already had quite a bit of photography experience, but the thought of going through an interview with the store manager who might ask him if he knew anything about jewelry (he didn't) and his lack of confidence had him more than a bit nervous.

It turned out that the store manager wanted someone who knew about cameras and photography. They had plenty of people who could sell jewelry. So, he got the job, leading to freelance photo gigs doing weddings, sports, and even some corporate jobs.

That first "real job" led to a full-time job as a reporter and photographer for the local paper. Later, while serving in the US Navy, he was quickly hired as a freelance photographer working for the largest newspaper in Virginia.

It will be different when you apply for a freelance position as an over-fifty-year-old. For starters, you have decades of experience, skill, and wisdom. "Been there, done that, got the t-shirt" applies to more than bungee jumping into the New River Gorge. You have an arsenal of tools at your disposal that puts you far ahead of the youngsters who may be competing for the same freelance jobs.

We were raised to have excellent ethics and values. As a group, people over 50 are reliable and dependable. We show up and do the work! We're more disciplined, responsible, and professional, and these characteristics make us stand out in today's workforce environment. There are several freelance employment sites, like Upwork and Fiverr, that let you bid on freelance jobs. You can find these in the **Resource Guide**. However, be aware that many (but not all) of the jobs on these platforms tend to be low paying or force you to compete against people in low and medium-income countries with lower living costs and who, therefore, can accept lower wages or fees.

If you sign up for a freelance site, you'll have to create a profile and possibly upload some samples of your work. In many ways, you can look at these sites as mini-social networks.

Once you have posted a profile and some content and your resume, you'll be visible to potential clients and able to search available postings. Again, it is a two-way street. Before you're hired, a virtual interview will occur as an online conversation that you'll have with the prospective client.

The more engaging and appealing you present yourself, the better your chances of finding success.

Freelance sites are less of an employment venue than a means of finding jobs or "gigs." You've probably heard references to the "gig economy." Freelance sites are how people participating in that economy find work and get paid for it.

Hang Out Your Own Shingle

Depending on your expertise, you could teach people a variety of skills.

Maybe you've become an expert at project management for small businesses and want to create an online course and offer classes. How to build the course, where to put it, what software to use, and how to sell and market it—all of this information is available on the Internet. You can search it out yourself if you're a DIYer; you can take on-line courses or hire someone to build and help you launch it. Alternatively, you can look for firms that offer training and are looking for "consultants" to provide that training. These are actual businesses that are always looking for people to perform training on their behalf. Training and education companies are excellent sources for a variety of skill sets.

It will take time, imagination, and some financial resources. However, if you use the experience and positive work traits you've accumulated over the years, it's likely that the rewards will undoubtedly outweigh the investment.

"Getting Your Feet Wet" from an Entrepreneurial Perspective

Or you may find you've developed an interest in working for yourself and running your own business. People sometimes compensate for losing a job by starting a new company based on market conditions and demands that exist at that time. While this is also a topic that could comprise an entire book, here are just a few tips to allow you to reflect on these options before deciding to follow this route.

There are TONS of resources out there, and many are only a Google search away. Many people are very eager to give you advice on starting a business. Some want to charge you for that information, while others are willing to give it to you for free.

If you've never started a business before, we recommend looking at Seth Godin's altMBA program or Steve Dotto's *Grey Wave* (a membership site). Going through these programs can help you "get your feet wet" in a new field by preparing you for what's to come. It will also give some idea of the challenges you may face as well as how to resolve them. The thing to remember is that while you may have a burning passion for getting started NOW, it's always helpful to do a little research and get some training before you jump in with both feet. No one has ever regretted doing preliminary research before starting a new project, much as you do when you prepare for a job interview.

International Working and Living

Have you wondered what it might be like to live and work in another country?

There's never been an easier time to do both. Bob's wife has relatives who moved to Thailand to work and live. They're the children of ex-pats who had moved to Australia a generation earlier from Ireland and Great Britain. They love living and working in Thailand! When we started checking out the idea of doing something similar, we learned that there was plenty of help out there to help you both move and find a job.

International Living is probably the best-known resource for moving, living, and working in another country. According to a November 9, 2020 article on their website,

> *"There is no shortage of spots where a retired couple can live well on $2,000 a month. You'll find good-quality medical care, exciting new traditions and cultures, great food fresh from the market, engaging ex-pat communities, welcoming locals, and more.*
>
> *"You can also find good value real estate in many locations around the world, whether your dream home is a house or a condo on the beach in the tropics, a resorted farmhouse in the country, or a home in a quiet mountain European village."*

What about working while living abroad? Most countries don't want you taking a job from a local resident. Others will allow certain occupations that are needed in their particular country. Teaching English to residents is welcome in Spain, Japan, China, Thailand, Italy, and many other countries. There are often certifications that need to be completed and rules to follow. However, it is an excellent way to "wet your toes" while working in other countries. And, after working for a year or two, you may find your ideal place to spend the rest of your life.

But there are plenty of other ways to continue to generate an income while living abroad.

Here Are Some Suggestions From International Living

You essentially sit at a desk in many jobs and interact with colleagues or customers via email, phone, instant message, or other online communication. Face-to-face meetings are rare.

1. **In that case, why not do it from a location overseas?** During the pandemic, while people worked remotely, they realized that they could work from anywhere with a good Internet connection. Some people left big cities for island paradises—whether temporarily or permanently. With high-speed Internet available just about everywhere, it's not complicated. What about meetings? You could join in via video conference with software like Zoom, Skype or through a teleconference line. One other advantage of working remotely: No one knows your age! They only care about your capabilities.

2. **You could work online as a freelancer.** You could take the skills you have now and start offering your services as a freelancer or consultant. You can work online with clients around the world. You could even take on a new skill. Some examples of promising freelance careers include proofreading and editing, content writing for websites, copywriting (advertising writing), graphic design, website design, and many more. You could also be a virtual assistant, which is like being an administrative assistant but remotely helping someone organize their business and schedule. You find these jobs through referrals or online job sites like Upwork.

3. **Rent out your home.** One easy way to make an extra income, or in some cases cover all your expenses, is by renting out of your home in the U.S. short-term through sites like Airbnb or long-term to renters who take out a year or multi-year lease. In this case, you would have to own your home, of course. Also, it's best to have a property manager handle bookings, check-ins, and maintenance on the property. They'll get a cut of the rental income in exchange for their services.

4. **You could start an online business.** You could take something you're an expert on or have an interest in and transform that into a business selling products online. For example, you could sell products on Amazon as an affiliate (see "How to Become an

Amazon Affiliate" in the **Resource Guide**), which means advertising products on behalf of a larger company. When you make a sale, you get a commission, which means you never actually have to ship the products or handle refunds or customer service. You could also create your own digital products like guides, videos, or online courses based on interest or expertise. These products you would sell to customers as digital downloads from your website or platforms like that.

5. **You could start a brick-and-mortar business.** If you've always dreamed of owning a restaurant or beach bar paradise, a clothing boutique, an ice cream shop, or any of many other businesses, you could start one overseas. In many countries, the cost to start and operate a business is much lower compared to the United States. There's often less red tape, too.

CHAPTER SEVEN

Learn to Manage Your Time

We reviewed a survey of Baby Boomers and Gen Xers we conducted who were looking at reentering the job market and went through their comments about what they found challenging. Over and over again, the same topic came up: time management. Many people in their 50s or older are worried that they aren't managing their time well. The thing about time management is that it isn't difficult. It just requires two things: organization and repetition.

But time management can be challenging even when you have just one job. If you're juggling your current job with a side job or a job search, or you're trying to start a side business while still bringing home a steady income, things can become complicated. Many people have trouble balancing the need to make a living with the need to start or switch to something new. The thing is, those same basic principles—organization and repetition—are the secret to juggling more than one job, managing a challenging schedule without losing your mind, and doing this all without working yourself to death.

Get Organized

If you've got a lot to do, your only choice is to be very organized. Fortunately, there are endless ways to stay organized in our modern era. You could use a paper calendar if you're the sort of person who needs to visually look at his or her tasks. You could keep any number of online task lists and calendars (Google offers both a calendar and a task list that is integrated into its email). You can use a smartphone or even a purpose-built electronic organizer.

Apps such as Evernote, Trello, Asana, and other productivity apps are free (for their basic versions), help keep track of different elements of a project or process and are an excellent first step to keeping organized. Evernote, in particular, is a place to "dump your brain" and not have to search for the same information over and over constantly. Asana and Trello will help you manage your projects, whether it's a new business, side hustle, or just finding a new job.

What you CAN'T do is try to remember *everything* off the cuff and expect to accomplish it all. You'll end up missing things and, the busier you get, the more harried you'll feel. Getting busier DEMANDS that you get organized.

One of the busiest people we know is a writer who works multiple freelance jobs at any given time. He has meetings with various clients and has numerous deadlines to meet. To keep track of it all, he prefers Google's email and productivity apps, like the calendar and task list, because they can be integrated and used on his Android phone. This means that he knows which tasks he must complete each day. He sets reminders for himself for things that must be tackled and sets up multiple early reminders for tasks that span a period of time and are about to become critical (in case he hasn't had time to handle them yet).

As long as he has Internet access, he'll know what he must do each day. Because he's so busy, he's also unfailingly reliable. Even if he runs late on a particular job, he'll *know* that he's running late and can let his client know he needs more time. If you and he were to arrange to meet at 3:15 p.m. at the local grocery store on August 21st, three years from now, you could be sure that he'll be there. He epitomizes the old saying, "If you want something done, give it to a busy person."

Whatever organization system you choose is up to you, but you MUST get organized so you can keep track of what's on your plate and how it all fits together. Whether it's a whiteboard in your kitchen, a desk blotter calendar in your office, or any of a million different smartphone applications, the next critical step is repetition once you've set up the system.

Repetition And Follow-Through

You need to have the discipline to keep repeating the steps we've discussed and then follow through on them. If you set a bunch of To-Do reminders for yourself for tomorrow but don't perform any of those tasks, then having a list of what you need to accomplish doesn't do you any good. Discipline is crucial if you're going to juggle multiple tasks and manage your time correctly. So make sure that you both organize and follow through on your organization. Keep track of your progress every day.

The system isn't magic. Things don't get done by themselves. If you set too ambitious a pace for yourself, you'll quickly burn out. If you try to accomplish too much, you'll either be miserable, or you won't get it done. Neither option is a formula for success. That's why you've also got to...

Know Your Limits

The third component of time management requires being realistic with your goals. Understand that while you're setting tasks for yourself, you also need to budget time to relax. It may sound silly to "schedule" time to relax, but if you don't do it, you'll go crazy.

The writer who uses Google to track all his tasks regularly schedules what he calls "couch time"—time to do nothing. He'll make an exception to these scheduled downtimes if it's necessary to get an urgent project done, but typically he sticks to it, so he doesn't burn out. This isn't laziness; it's making sure that you don't work yourself so hard that you can't get ANY work done.

Have you ever worked so hard you got sick? Getting sick is your body's way of FORCING you to rest. Especially these days, you can't afford to do that to yourself. So while you're organizing your time and being disciplined to stick to your schedule and execute your tasks on an ongoing basis, always leave time to relax and rest. You'll be happier and, more importantly, you'll get MORE work done over time than if you push yourself too hard, which you may regret later.

CHAPTER EIGHT

Be Open to Unexpected Solutions

No matter what you want to do, a significant hurdle to achieving success isn't something shared by just Boomers and Gen Xers alone. It is something that all human beings tend to do, and that's artificially constraining your options.

Here's how it happens: You lose your job, and you look for a new one. But as you view each job prospect, you come up with reasons why it isn't an option: this one pays too little, that one is too far away, this one is too similar to a previous job that you didn't like, that one probably won't hire you because it's an industry that favors young people and you don't think you'd do well there, and so on. Instead of trying and seeing how things work out, you filter your options and discard a bunch of them. This means that you're missing out on all kinds of opportunities.

People often do this when it comes to major life decisions. We all resist change, so we find excuses for not doing something. For example, have you ever considered moving to take advantage of new job opportunities? Most of us don't; we have a laundry list of reasons why, so we never even try.

Baby Boomers and Gen Xers are especially susceptible to this natural tendency to constrain our possible solutions. The older we get, the more reluctant we are to make significant life changes. You may have specific requirements for what a job *should* be like or *should* involve, and as you look at the market, those "shoulds" stop you from finding ANY job. We're not saying that you should work at a job you hate. Still, you should be willing to step outside of your established habits and patterns rather than dismissing solutions that are workable (even if they're unexpected or unusual).

For example, Bob knows a woman who worked in IT for many, many years. When the dot-com bubble burst, she was out of a job and middle-aged. And because of the unique circumstances that allowed her to work her way up in the IT job she'd held for years, she lacked a lot of the certifications that would make her marketable to a new company today. She spent 18 months trying to get a new job in IT but kept coming up empty. With her unemployment payments running out, she had to make a decision.

She decided to completely and utterly change careers. She went to Truck Driving school, earned a commercial driver's license, and today is one of those truckers with over a million miles logged. Not only does she love her new job and can't imagine going back to IT work, but she's now also working in an industry in which, if she were to lose her job tomorrow, she could immediately be hired to do the same thing for another company. (Truck drivers are that high in demand).

To make this change, she had to completely change her attitude about being away from home during the week. As it turned out, though, her personality type really enjoys that kind of freedom. She couldn't be happier in her career now, and it's all because she was willing to embrace an unusual, unfamiliar solution.

What are unusual solutions available to you? What could you discover if only you stopped constraining what you'd be willing to consider?

CHAPTER NINE

Your Appearance Speaks Before You Do

We won't spend a lot of time on this, and our generations aren't usually the worst offenders in this area, but it merits mentioning because it's so often repeated. Over and over again, job-hunting tips mention "appearance." You may be thinking that this is for younger people who don't seem to understand what it means to dress up for things, and yes, our society has gotten more casual over the years. But the ugly little truth is that it's not unusual for us to let ourselves go a bit as we get older.

You've heard this before: "You never get a second chance to make a first impression." And as COVID-19 changed interviewing for a job from in-person to online, an excellent first impression now is often going to occur by video conferencing. Even as the world "opens up" and we start having face-to-face meetings again, you may find that at least your initial interviews will be virtual, over the webcam on your computer or your phone. So, spend some time learning how to set up your camera correctly, make sure you have good lighting, have the videoconference take place in a clean room, and maintain a presentable appearance.

Think about the person interviewing you. They may interview 20-30 people for a job, and half of them have poor internet connections. Their video looks terrible, and the audio breaks up and makes them difficult to understand. So, the interviewer comes away with a poor impression. People enjoy visiting with someone who has a good-quality connection, right? So, think of this as showing up with clean and polished shoes.

It's a pleasure to speak with somebody who clearly understands how to use the technology and demonstrates respect for the interviewer.

FIVE TIPS FOR BETTER VIDEO CONFERENCING

1. Sound

Audio is the most important part of any Video Conference. You can have a successful call if your video sucks, but bad audio is the kiss of death.

Get a good Mic, a decent USB Mic can be purchased for $80, if you do not want to make the investment, make sure you are using a set of earbuds (like from your phone).

Headphones or earbuds also overcome the challenge of echo or feedback.

2. **Lighting**

Spending a few minutes thinking about lighting will make a bigger difference in your video quality than buying a new camera.

Natural light is best, situating your setup in front of a window that will flood you with natural light is a perfect setup.

If a window is not convenient, various LED video lights from small "selfie" lights to larger kits will make a huge difference in how you look on camera.

3. **Distraction**

Your background says a lot about you.

Think about what our parents taught us about job interviews, dressing for the role, having polished shoes.

Your background in a video conference will tell the others if you are neat or sloppy, in control or out of control in your personal life.

If possible, a clean and organized background will serve you well.

We are not a fan of virtual backgrounds unless you invest in a proper green screen setup.

4. Bandwidth

Avoid choppy connections:

Turn off Dropbox or other automatic syncing.

Ask your family to stay offline during the call, NO NETFLIX!

Close unnecessary apps and browser tabs on your computer.

5. Interruptions

Turn off notifications on your computer, silence your phone, close the door and tell your family to respect your need for quiet.

As a result of the pandemic many companies have discovered that employees can be just as effective working from home without the need for brick-and-mortar office buildings. We predict that many of us will find the daily commute to the office a thing of the past, which will make the need to understand technology even more critical.

CHAPTER TEN

Be Flexible with Your Job Description and Salary Requirements and Dealing With Adversity

---

Before we get into where we go from here, it's important to talk about having inflexible job or salary requirements. It's not unusual for people who've been in the working world for a long time to have a very defined idea of what they're worth. The problem is that when you switch jobs or change careers entirely, you may "price yourself out of the market" by insisting on a salary that the market won't bear. This could leave you unemployed.

Looking for a new job is a challenge at any time, but especially during this pandemic. The good news is there are lots of companies looking for people with experience. The not-so-good news is that older workers who lost their jobs in previous difficult financial times are disproportionately impacted. According to the Urban Institute, history shows that once the labor market picks up and employers begin rehiring, older workers will find themselves near the back of the line. After the Great Recession, workers ages 62 and older were about half as likely to become reemployed as their counterparts ages 25 to 34. And when unemployed older workers found a new job, they earned barely half as much as they did on their previous job.[7]

The first thing you need to do is recognize that you may have to accept a salary that you believe is beneath you or not what you expected. This is what's necessary to get your foot in the door. As you work your way up, you'll be able to negotiate better terms. Being willing to accept a lower salary or what you consider an "entry-level" job can make a difference in the long run.

A good friend was employed by a company for 20 years and worked her way up to the number two spot where she was running the day-to-day operations. Then, without much notice, the company was sold. She was offered the same position with the new company—but with a 35% cut in salary. She either had to find new employment or accept the cut. Being over 60, she chose to accept the position at a much lower wage. But guess what? She's fantastic at her job, and the new owners

---

7 https://www.urban.org/urban-wire/unemployment-surges-older-workers-need-more-help

quickly realized that they had a gem of a new employee. They began compensating her with bonuses and other profit-sharing tools.

The other thing you can do is completely change the game. We previously mentioned the "gig economy" and taking on freelance work. There are all kinds of new ways to make money, such as driving for Uber or Lyft, that weren't available when we were younger. You can change careers (like the IT woman who became a truck driver) or go into a different field entirely. Your physical limitations may constrain some of your options—for example if you can't stand for 12 hours a day, then working as a security guard is not the job for you—but many other options simply didn't exist twenty years ago.

Here's an example of being willing to take a job you think is beneath you: The father of a friend of Bob's was an engineer for many years before starting his own business. He became a technical writer, and for years enjoyed an affluent lifestyle. He was his own boss, and at the height of his success, had two employees working for him.

Then disaster struck. His primary client folded up shop, and because he hadn't been developing new clients, he ended up deeply in debt. He ended up having to sell his dream house and look for work with an employer again after spending years as his own boss. He complained bitterly about having to "work for someone else," but he swallowed his pride and took a job as a technical writer for a local industrial company.

He thought the salary was beneath him given what he had been making as his own boss, but something happened that he hadn't expected. He thrived. The stress of running his own business had always been difficult. Working for a salary again left him free to focus on the basics of doing his job without taking the stress home with him. Now that he was living in a modest townhouse and not investing in his own business, the new salary turned out to be quite adequate, too.

He worked until retirement age, sold most of his possessions, and bought a camper so he could travel the country—something he'd always wanted to do. Because he had to take a job he thought was beneath him, he was able to accomplish and enjoy one of his life's goals.

Dealing With Adversity: The Unforeseen Scenario

As you already understand, it can be challenging to achieve your goals at any point in your life, and perhaps even more so (though not impossible) when you do it as an older person. But something happened not long before this book was written that changed how we ALL looked at the world. That was a disruption, something none of us anticipated but which had far-reaching implications for the entire world. While things like this have happened before, and some were pretty serious (such as the dot-com bubble bursting or the housing collapse and 2008 recession), none was as powerful as the disruption caused by the COVID-19 pandemic.

COVID-19 and the Great 2020 Disruption

The pandemic began in late 2019 and spread to the rest of the world in 2020. Fear of the virus and the illness and death tolls associated with it drove a panic that caused most of the world (with a few notable exceptions) to go into "lockdown."

Those quarantines, in which all but "essential" workers were told to stay home except for trips to the grocery store, pharmacy, etc., caused the economy to collapse. The robust American economy suddenly started charting record unemployment. This was because people who had jobs were told they couldn't work at them while government printing presses churned out money to distribute massive stimulus and unemployment payments.

This disruption caused a lot of people to be displaced from their jobs. Anyone who couldn't work from home, and any business that couldn't conduct business by delivery or curbside pickup, was dead in the water. This was a stark wake-up call for many people who thought their jobs were secure or who never suspected they would end up unemployed. But in this adversity, something amazing happened. People learned to adapt, and they started making money again.

What We Can Learn From the Pandemic Disruption

The examples are endless. All you need to do is look around. Do some searching online for companies that dealt with adversity during the pandemic. See the types of solutions they employed. You'll be amazed and heartened by how they chose to overcome these problems to continue making a living. It all comes down to diversifying your income streams so that the loss of any one of them can't destroy your livelihood.

The businesses that failed during the Great Disruption were those that relied on in-person point-of-sale transactions, in-person interaction, and to a lesser extent, disposable income. The pandemic was an unforeseen external force that disrupted specific jobs and the means of acquiring income in ways we couldn't anticipate. People who had worked their entire lives as bartenders and servers and had enjoyed a kind of job security (because there would always be jobs for experienced servers, right?) discovered that with lockdowns and quarantine, they could no longer work the jobs at which they excelled. What were they to do? They learned, as did so many other workers worldwide, that building a resilient career to disruptions requires having multiple income streams (from different sources such as a side hustle) and a certain amount of flexibility when it comes to how you get your work done.

You Need Multiple Income Streams (Money Is Power Is Freedom)

No matter what you do, it's helpful to develop alternative income streams that are different from your primary source of income. They must be different enough so that there's a chance you'll survive even if other streams completely stop producing revenue.

Money is power and freedom. The more money you have coming in from different sources, the better off you'll be. If you have several different part-time jobs, each of which generates income, then if one job is disrupted, you can still make some money. The more diverse your income streams, the better off you will be.

We know of several people working various service-industry jobs (such as servers and bartenders) who also do freelance writing, copyediting, and virtual assistant work through Fiverr and Upwork. When the lockdowns closed all the restaurants and bars, those same employees expanded their work on their freelance jobs.

When the world's governments, notably the United States, started recommending and even mandating masks, there was a massive demand for surgical masks and even cloth face coverings. People with a sewing machine and basic skills began producing and selling masks on Etsy and local websites. Suddenly, Etsy's home page was wall-to-wall masks. The makers filled the gap before commercial suppliers caught up with demand.

Four months after the start of the pandemic, every drugstore had disposable surgical masks for sale, but until then, it was Etsy's makers (and makers from other sites) who made a small fortune. They weren't price-gouging; they were simply producing a product that was high in demand.

This situation is different from starting your own business or side hustle. This was a one-time opportunity that people grabbed to stay afloat financially until their jobs returned or they found new employment. The lesson in this example is the more sources of income you have, the better off you will be.

For example, you could drive for Uber or Lyft to produce an alternate income stream (although working for both at the same time provides an essentially identical income stream). When California passed a law that threatened to put ridesharing out of business, anyone working for Uber who also worked for Lyft could not use one to supplement the other. But if you were a taxi driver who drove for Uber or Lyft on the side, your job with the taxi company was safe in California. (The state subsequently saw the passage of Proposition 22 with heavy support from Uber and Lyft that reclassified "gig economy drivers" as a new category of worker—not a freelancer, not an employee, but an independent contractor.) The new law has some issues, and critics claim the ride-sharing companies essentially "bought" the law. Regardless, it meant that drivers for ride-sharing companies could continue to make money in California.

You can never predict what's going to happen in the future, from a global pandemic to a dumb law meant to protect freelancers from exploitation (**AB5**)[8] that ended up putting them out of business. That's why diversifying your income streams is so important. (It's just like diversifying your investments, so you don't have all your eggs in one basket.) The more income streams you have, and the more different they are from each other, the better off you'll be.

You Need Income Streams You Can Maintain From Home (or Wherever)

The other huge lesson of the pandemic was, of course, that being able to work from home (or anywhere else) conferred to those employees a HUGE advantage. This means that whenever possible, try to arrange your job(s) circumstances so that you can perform them remotely. With modern video conferencing, virtual private networks, and specific other equipment and software, most jobs can be performed from anywhere. If your job requires specialized equipment that remains on-site, consider setting up a home version of the same equipment.

---

8 California Assembly Bill 5 (AB5) is a controversial piece of legislation that requires California employers to classify independent contractors as "employees" if certain conditions are met.
https://www.nolo.com/legal-encyclopedia/california-gig-worker-law-AB-5.html

If you work in an office, make sure that early on that you inquire about and set up the necessary systems to work from a remote location if need be. In the past, this was harder to request than it is these days.

It's worth planning ahead to make sure you can still perform your job even when you're not at the physical location. After all, now that the world has experienced these long-term lockdowns, it's not unthinkable that our governments will turn to them again should the pandemic surge again (or another unanticipated situation arises).

Stockpile Supplies/Inventory

You may think of stockpiling supplies and inventory as something only self-employed people need to worry about. Still, it's something you need to consider for any freelance job or "side hustle." This even applies to direct employment jobs where you're required to keep certain supplies on hand. Especially during the 2020 pandemic's days of "broken" or "disrupted" supply chains, establishing multiple methods for obtaining your inventory and shipping out products to customers is vital. If your employer, freelance business, or side hustle needs inventory or requires that you ship a physical product, you can't afford to rely on only one service (like the United States Post Office).

During the pandemic, we saw the Post Office and sites like Amazon become highly strained. At one point,

Amazon stopped shipping all but "essential" products and put long delays on delivering other merchandise. A colleague told Bob that he bought almost everything he needed from decentralized eBay sellers during the worst month or two of the pandemic quarantine because he could get the merchandise faster.

The Post Office began having real problems during that same period due to the demand placed by the pandemic and the national election. Deliveries were delayed by weeks and even months, in some cases. Packages went missing, too. It is an excellent idea to establish accounts with alternative shippers if the job or freelance gig you desire means you'll be shipping or receiving products. You need to know that if one of your means of shipping and fulfillment becomes unreliable or unavailable, you have other options.

Ensure Shipping Flexibility

The U.S. postal service is losing money and could go out of business entirely. It is close to being insolvent and may have to privatize or cut back on services. If you don't have another way to ship products to your customers, you'll be out of luck. You would do well to explore options like UPS and FedEx and obtain the supplies you'll need ahead of time. This type of shipping flexibility is now more critical than ever because the pandemic showed us just how close our postal service came to the breaking point.

Of course, alternative services are vulnerable, too. If there's a strike at UPS, for example, you had better have a FedEx account, and so on. Always have fallback options. Flexibility is the name of the game.

Improvise, Adapt, Overcome

One of the positive things that came out of the pandemic was seeing the many ways businesses overcame their challenges and adapted to keep earning money despite the restrictions on in-person service. In one state, food deliveries were allowed while dining in was not. One enterprising strip club started having their dancers deliver food to order so they could remain open.

An Internet marketer who sells a variety of physical products found its supply lines from China shut down. He couldn't get more inventory and couldn't sell some of his most profitable items—bags used for survival kits. When he couldn't get those anymore, he pivoted to digital-information products—eBooks that contained survival information his customers would want.

Digital Products and Online Delivery

The pandemic was a HUGE boon to digital-product sellers and those offering online delivery. Kindle books had been outselling paperbacks before 2020 but buying electronic books online couldn't be affected by lockdowns and quarantines. Amazon made a fortune during this time, some of it coming from books and videos. And speaking of videos, the movie industry experimented with at-home delivery of new-release movies. Because people were starved for entertainment, those companies, too, broke sales records and made a fortune.

Diversifying Your Income Streams (The Need For "Side Hustles")

This topic could be an entire book (and, in fact, is a book that Bob wrote right before the pandemic called *"Now, Not Later: Make More Money Immediately."*). It's simply common sense to have something to fall back on. The next challenges we face will be ones we cannot predict. Thus, it makes sense to start side jobs that can generate money. Now you may say, "That's fine, but I can't take on multiple jobs without working myself to death." That's true. The key is to identify a way to make a little money on side hustles that you could scale up in an emergency. For example, one of our technical writing contacts runs a resume-writing business. It is not the primary focus of his business. Still, when he needs more money (especially when the economy takes a downturn, which generates demand for updated resumes), he starts advertising his resume-writing service to bring in more business.

You, too, can maintain multiple small side hustles that can be scaled up or down as needed. For example, Etsy allows shop owners to switch off the shop to "go on vacation," while eBay sellers have a very similar option that tells buyers they are "away" for a set time. Similarly,

Uber and Lyft drivers only get calls for their services when they are logged in to the app.

Features like these enable you to work when you want to work but take breaks when working your side hustle is not your primary focus.

Nobody predicted the 2020 pandemic. Yes, we knew the danger of a global pandemic was out there, and there had been earlier scares with SARS, MERS, and the Swine Flu, but we never faced anything approaching the disruption caused by COVID-19. No one was ready for it.

By definition, the next challenge will also be something we cannot "specifically" predict. Survivalists talk about the concept of "anti-fragility," which refers to setting up your life and in this case, your job or jobs to be resistant to breaking in a way that allows you to benefit if something terrible happens. If you arrange your work so that you can perform it from anywhere, source your business and personal supplies from multiple outlets, and pivot to meet new and unforeseen demands, you'll be "anti-fragile." This will allow you to handle any new challenge you face, even without knowing what it might be.

CHAPTER ELEVEN

You Still Have Time - Achieving Your Life Goals

You still have time to do things you haven't done. Your goals are possible and achievable. Your dreams are ready to materialize. You have years of relationships and connections who will support you. Throughout history, elders have been respected for their wisdom and life experiences. This is your time!

> **"YOU STILL HAVE TIME TO DO THINGS YOU HAVEN'T DONE."**

What Haven't You Done?

Do you feel like you've "gotten old" without doing the things you wanted to do? What contributed to why you feel you haven't achieved what you wanted? Did your career path not go as you had wanted or planned? Whatever it is, the time to make a change is NOW. Pitying yourself won't get the job done. Do you know what your goals are, or do you just feel dissatisfied?

Here's a way to figure it out:

First, make a list of the things you're HAPPY about. You must do this on paper or the screen of a word-processing program—not just in your head.

Now, make a list of things you're UNHAPPY about.

Finally, make a list of the things you want to do but haven't done.

Now compare the lists. How different is the list of what you want to do compared with the things in your UNHAPPY list?

Now, look at all the lists together. What patterns jump out at you? What does this little bit of self-reflection tell you about where you've been, where you're going, and where you would LIKE to be going? It should point you to **what you want to do**. And you still have time to do it!

You're About to Make Some Changes

Change makes people uneasy. It makes friends, family, and coworkers very nervous. That's okay. But understand that what you're about to do is going to shake things up a bit.

What you DON'T want to do is give in to a "midlife crisis" of wallowing in regret and starting to alienate people. Facing change and feeling our mortality can be overwhelming at times. But, this is also the perfect time to create more meaning in your life. What you're about to do won't be a quick fix (what thing worth accomplishing ever is?). Instead, you need to identify the "rest of your life goals" and start making gradual changes to attain those goals.

Understand, though, that not everyone will be supportive and understanding. Doing something without universal agreement and approval isn't the same as alienating or cutting yourself off from the people around you. At times you'll need to walk a fine line between the two. But what you need to do now is sit down and make a list of the goals you can realistically achieve based on what you've learned from your three-list comparison.

View Your Goals and Life Changes
REALISTICALLY

Retake a look at your lists. What are the top three goals based on what's most important to you, realistic, and viable (meaning that you can afford to do it based on either cost or likely income)? Are these goals achievable within your financial means? If so, how? If not, what do you need to do to make them possible, or what else could you do that would be achievable?

With your top three "realistically achievable" goals in mind, start making a list of what you need to do to achieve those goals. If you can work on those goals without completely upending your life—go for it! If you feel more comfortable taking these steps slowly, there would be nothing wrong with approaching the changes cautiously. The changes don't have to be made at once; big dreams usually aren't accomplished overnight. You're a Boomer or Gen Xer—not The Mummy with one foot in the grave. You've got some time to get things done without completely upending the apple cart, as they say.

You Can Succeed

There's an old saying we always return to: "The journey of a thousand miles begins with a single step." It sounds a little trite, but it's absolutely true.

Here's an example from a more contemporary source: In the Marvel Universe movie, "Doctor Strange," Benedict Cumberbatch played an arrogant doctor who spent his entire life working to become one of the best surgeons in the world. When an accident damaged his hands, his search for a mystical solution took him to the wise and powerful monks in Tibet (or someplace like that). When they showed him that magic and sorcery were possible, he lit up. *This* was what he'd always wanted to do, although he never knew it. But how, he asked, could he get from where he was—disabled and penniless—to what he wanted to become: a powerful master sorcerer?

"How did you become a doctor?" the Ancient One (the wise, seemingly all-powerful teacher) asks.

"Study and practice," says Dr. Strange. "Years of it."

The audience is then treated to a montage of Strange learning his new skills from books and devouring knowledge that is presented to him. He learns that he can be something he didn't even know he wanted to be, and he does it by leveraging a skill he already has—the ability to study.

As a Boomer or Gen Xer, you've lived through good times and bad. You've been around long enough to know that things don't always go as you want. You've got enough life experience under your belt to know that sometimes you'll fail and have to start over. And you also know that if you just put your mind to something and work hard at it, you'll achieve it. You're not afraid of hard work; you've got a better work ethic than most of the people around you.

In other words, you're poised for success. You deserve to have what you want. You deserve to achieve what you want to achieve. Use the information in this book as a starting point—and then get out there and make your future happen!

You can do it. We know you can. We know it because we did it, too.

CHAPTER TWELVE

What's Next? Your Plan of Action

Once you've had a chance to digest everything you've learned up to this point—about yourself, the world in which you'll be looking for work or starting a business, the obstacles you'll face— then what? Having learned in these pages what *not* to do, it's time to implement your plan based on what you *should, will,* and *must* do. Don't worry; it isn't difficult. That doesn't mean it won't involve hard work, but it's easy to understand and follow, step by step. And, hey, you're a Boomer or Gen Xer; you're not afraid of hard work.

Right about now, you're asking yourself, "Okay, how do I start?" This is where we implement a plan of action. Based on what you've read so far, you understand the basics of how to overcome the hurdles you face. It's time to put your plan into action. Don't worry if you don't have a specific plan in mind because we've created the roadmap for you. These are the basic, conceptual steps. You can implement them one at a time and move forward.

It's a good idea to get "old school" with your plan of action. Get out of a pad of paper and a pen or pencil and start jotting down notes. This will become your guidebook for moving forward. Remember, this is a Big Step. You've done it before, but that was a long time ago. You're out of practice, so take it one step at a time and cut yourself a lot of slack along the way. You're embarking on a process to change your life. You should have a smile on your face as you contemplate what you'll do next and as you take action to implement it.

Given all that, here's what to do, step by step:

1. **Assess your Skills.**

   What can you do? What are you willing to try? What skills do you need to develop, and can you do it on your own, or will you need to search for a course, teacher, mentor, etc.? What training is available to help you learn the new skills? These are all questions you need to ask yourself when looking to change jobs or start a new income stream. Every plan of action begins with realistically assessing your skills and taking stock of what's available to you as well as what you need to accomplish to achieve your goals.

2. *Prepare Your Resume and Establish Your Social Media Profiles*

Do you have an up-to-date resume that conforms to the guidelines we've described in this book? If not, take the time to create one (or pay someone to create it for you). We have provided several sample resume templates after the **Resource Guide** section of this book.

Once your resume is in order, make sure you've established an essential social media presence by creating your social media profiles. We've already discussed the range of social media in which you may want to establish a presence, but LinkedIn and Facebook are good starting points. Joyce Feustal offers her own LinkedIn Profile as an example of how to create yours, which you can view **Resource Guide**. She also provides tips for enhancing your LinkedIn Profile in "What Are the Best Ways to Enhance a LinkedIn Profile."

3. *Set Up Your Job/Hunting Schedule*

If you're unemployed and looking for a job, finding your next job IS your job now. Treat it as such. If you're also starting a side hustle or trying to change career paths, you'll have less time available to job hunt. Either way, the only way to effectively manage your time is to be highly organized. Prepare a schedule of job-hunting tasks that include websites to visit, calls to make, companies to make inquiries, etc. Set up your budget, allowing a realistic amount of time to accomplish specific tasks. Create a To-Do List for each day and then stick to your schedule. If you find you weren't realistic in establishing your schedule, revise it, but once you have a realistic timeline set, stick to it.

4. Implement Your Schedule and Be Consistent

Here is the most challenging part: Once you have a schedule, STICK TO IT. Make sure you don't treat it as "optional." With your list of websites, tasks, and resume detailing your accomplishments prepared, the hard part is done. Now the day-to-day work of being consistent and following through begins. Follow your schedule and make sure you don't get complacent. The only way to accomplish your list of tasks is by sticking to it.

You can automate this process by using Google Tasks, Google Calendar, or other applications that help you track what's on your plate. Check out Evernote. Evernote is designed for taking notes, organizing, task management, and archiving. Steve calls it his "brain." There's a free **Evernote Quick Start Guide** on Steve's website and in our **Resource Guide**. Bob found it years ago, started using Evernote, and realized that this DottoTech guy knew his stuff! From that, a friendship and this book developed.

This raises a critical question: **What if you start feeling discouraged?** It's only natural to feel discouraged along the way, but we need to talk about that as it can destroy your follow-through. According to the AARP, the average time for someone our age to get a new job is now over one year (but that statistic is based on *everyone* our age looking for a job). By putting into action the ideas in this book, you will have the advantage!

Here's a way to avoid that feeling: Break each task down to its smallest component. Let's say you've targeted a particular company. You may have even heard about a job you think you'd like to pursue. So, instead of writing down a To-Do item like "Contact XYZ company about a job," break it down into to steps. For example, dependent upon the type of job and company you want to take these actions:

- Research XYZ Company
- What do they currently sell?
- Where and who is their market?
- What's the latest news about them?
- Is their business changing?
- Do I know anyone who works there?
- Who are their main competitors, partners, even vendors? (You may already have a contact with a vendor or partner who can introduce/ refer you.)

* Do I know someone who can introduce me to someone who works there to learn more about the company?

* Find out the name of the person to contact regarding the job I want.

* Who else should I talk to there?

   Breaking down challenging assignments into smaller tasks allows you to check off items on your To-Do list. This will give a sense of accomplishment and momentum, which may be hard to feel if you're looking at one BIG To Do item.

5. **Persist.**

Yes, this is an actual step. Job hunting can take months or even longer, depending on what you're trying to accomplish. You have to remember this and not let it get you down. Don't give up. Keep going!

As you might imagine, following through is the most challenging part here. People often "fail" when they try something new. "New" things can be hard, and when we encounter difficult things, we may be tempted to give up. We tell ourselves that what we're pursuing isn't right for us anyway, and we're not cut out for it. It isn't meant to be. This is when you have to reach deep down into yourself and remind yourself of your past accomplishments. Were you always confident that you could achieve the tasks ahead of you? I thought not. But, you succeeded more often than you failed. We know this to be a fact because you would not have read this far if it were not.

TIPS FOR FOLLOW-THROUGH

Initiative and Drive:

There's an old episode of *The Simpsons* in which Homer, who hates his job, finds himself trapped in that job. He needs the money, but some circumstances prevent him from leaving his job. It would be easy for him to become apathetic and despondent (which is kind of his natural state, anyway). Instead, he creates a sign with a slogan above his workstation that reads, "Do it for her." It reminds him that his motivation to do what he does is his infant daughter, Maggie. *She* is what prompts him, what *drives* him.

As part of your self-assessment—looking at yourself, your skills, your strength, your weaknesses—sit down and ask yourself, "What drives me? What sparks me to take the initiative, keep moving, and TRYING something new? What is my purpose, my prime motivator?" If it's money and commercial success, put up posters or pictures or clippings of the things you're working toward earning.

Affirmations that say things like "I WILL Do This" and "This Is Achievable" may sound corny, but they are helpful reminders. Your mindset toward your tasks will make all the difference in the world. A friend of Bob's related this story about six years ago:

> The friend was unemployed and deeply depressed because of it. His marriage had fallen apart, and he was worried about the relationship he might not get to have with his infant daughter. After a night of drinking alone in the small room he rented where he essentially lived "in exile" following the breakup of his marriage and the bankruptcy that followed, he woke up to discover that "everything smelled like booze." After wondering if he had spilled alcohol in literally every corner of the room, he realized that the smell was coming out of HIM.
>
> As he staggered into the bathroom to shower, he turned on a local AM radio station. The radio host talked about something that had recently happened in the news but then said, "What you need to do is stop feeling sorry for yourself. You need to pick

yourself up and dust yourself off and realize that feeling sorry won't change anything."

The friend said he looked at the radio and wondered, for a split second, if he'd gone mad. Taking it as a sign, he realized that, yes, all the drinking and self-pitying was not a formula for change. That day, after cleaning himself up, he sat down and determined what his strengths were. He formed a plan to borrow money to get certified as an armed guard so he could find employment and a new career.

But a funny thing happened after he started approaching life with a positive, goal-directed attitude: A job opportunity in his current profession fell into his lap. He interviewed for and got the job. He never borrowed the money or pursued the certification only because *he didn't need to*. He ended up working at his new place of employment for more than a decade after that fateful moment. Before that point, he'd never held a job for more than five years.

What changed? It was his attitude. It's very easy to fall into depression, self-pity, and apathy. But he realized that he had to make a change. His initiative and drive came from realizing that he would be a miserable failure if he didn't make a change. He also realized that he owed his daughter (who is now 12-years old and with whom he has a beautiful relationship) his best effort to provide for her and himself.

Holding Yourself Accountable

Revelations like the one above aside, there's another way to help drive yourself forward, and that is to hold yourself accountable. Make sure that the important people in your life know what you're doing. Share with them your efforts in meeting your goals. If you have a spouse, a close friend or partner, or someone else who wants to see you succeed, those are excellent choices for "accountability buddies."

This is the principle behind how diet apps encourage you to "friend" other people and share your progress with them. It's also why people work out or exercise with friends on a regular, scheduled basis so they won't be tempted to skip the gym or a jog. Being accountable to others helps drive you to keep up with your progress.

It's too easy to wallow in failure when nobody's looking. It's much harder to do that when people you care about and respect notice.

Just be sure to choose "accountability buddies" you trust. Some people will claim they want you to succeed but will undermine you out of jealousy. You don't need these types of superficial friends to be part of what you're doing.

Keeping Yourself On Track

What does it mean to keep yourself on track when pursuing your goals? It's a simple formula: Accountability = Repetition over time. Make a schedule, stick to it, achieve your daily goals, and repeat the process to achieve your longer-term goals.

An author we know says that nobody ever writes a novel. They write a chapter and then repeat the process. Well, staying on track is something you must do day after day. If you don't meet your goals today, that's fine; it happens. Just do your best to meet them tomorrow. Repeat the process every day. Put in the time and effort. Before you know it, you'll be succeeding through persistence because you stayed on track.

If these methods don't work to keep you on track, sit down and ask yourself, "Why?" Is your goal unrealistic? Have you tried to reach too far too fast? Is there something wrong with your goal? If you picked the right one, but something still isn't working, you need to assess why you're having so much trouble staying on your path. Whatever the reason, consult with someone who has accomplished what you want to do.

For example, if you're trying to change careers, find someone who is already in that career and chat with them about it. You'd be surprised how willing most people are to talk about themselves and what they do. You can find them on social media, among your friends or network, and in multiple other ways. After all, as a Boomer or Gen Xer, you've spent a lot more time accumulating contacts, right? There's no reason you shouldn't take advantage of that.

It's Time To Get Started

That's it. You've done it. You've reached the end of the book. So now what?

Are you going to put the book aside and change nothing, or will you implement the concrete plans contained within this book and achieve your goals?

We know that you may feel that you've been passed over, that society doesn't value its older citizens. At times you may even feel like you don't recognize the country you live in or the business you work in compared with what it was years ago. We get that because, at times, we've felt that way, too. You must remember that you are already a success! You've survived through decades of ups and downs and the very fact you're still alive and kicking today is proof you've made more right decisions than wrong ones.

The fact is you DESERVE to have what you want. You DESERVE to achieve what you want to achieve. There may be challenges along the way—in fact, there almost certainly will be—but these can be overcome. You have the tools and talent to overcome them. All you have to do is take the first step... then the next... and keep moving forward.

Use this book as a starting point. No, it doesn't contain ALL the answers because no single book could. But it does contain the essential plan, the essential components, for you to get where you want to go. That's our wish for you. Go forward, do what you want to do, get what you want, and most importantly, *be who you want to be.*

> "AGE APPEARS BEST IN FOUR THINGS: OLD WOOD TO BURN, OLD WINE TO DRINK, OLD FRIENDS TO TRUST, AND OLD AUTHORS TO READ."
> FRANCIS BACON

When you do that, you'll be living your best life, and you deserve to do that, too. It's not too late. You're not too old. Countless other people have done it.

You can, too.

Listen First – Sell Later®

– Bob Poole

Have fun storming the castle!

*–Miracle Max the Wizard,
The Princess Bride, and Steve Dotto*

RESOURCE GUIDE

For the latest Resource updates and additional helpful information, please check out our online guide at https://nolimitover50.com/resources or scan this QR Code.

Resume Creation and Writing Tips

1. Indeed Career Guide: It contains resumes and cover letter examples and tips.

2. Resume templates can be found at such sites as resume.io, resume-now.com, and many other locations.

3. The Free Resume Kit from AARP also provides everything you need to help you create an updated professional resume.

4. Here's an example of a Keyword Resume.

LinkedIn Profile

1. Joyce Feustel helps people, especially those age 55 and up, to become more effective at using social media, especially LinkedIn and Facebook. She works with business owners, business development professionals, business consultants, job seekers, and more, ranging from entrepreneurs to people in large corporations. Find her at Boomer Social Media Tutor.

2. Joyce Feustal's sample LinkedIn Profile

Online Resources to Find Employment

1. The AARP Job Board connects you with employers that value your experience.

2. "ThirdQuarter": An Online Job Service for Canadians.

3. AARP's Job Search Resources for 50+: The top online websites to help land your next job.

4. Workforce50 Jobs is a full-service job board where employers are looking specifically for older workers.

5. Nifty50s: Job Advice for People in their 50s.

Personal Website Templates

1. Templates for creating a personal website can be found at Wix.com, Canva.com, Imcreator.com, and other sites.

Freelance & Gigwork

1. Freelance jobs can be found on such websites as Upwork.com, Fiverr.com, FlexJobs, and even CraigsList.

2. Seth Godin's Freelancer Course

3. Learn How to Become an Amazon Affiliate.

4. Steady App - Find More Ways to Increase Your Income

Helpful Productivity Apps

1. Evernote, Asana, and Trello are apps that can help you organize and manage your time. Steve is an Evernote expert and has a free quick-start course you can check out.

Communication Skills

1. Urban Dictionary: is a crowdsourced online dictionary for slang words and phrases.

2. Effective Communication at Work: Speaking and Writing Well in the Modern Workplace by Vicki

McLeod. "In the digital age, as workers increasingly go remote, the ability to communicate clearly and effectively is—now more than ever—a highly desirable skill.

3. Improving Communication Skills

Learn New Skills

1. Learn just about any skills you'll need for your new job: Coursera, Skillshare, Udemy, Lifehack.org.

2. Steve Dotto's Evernote Quick Start Guide: This course will help you master the Evernote basics in the easiest, most efficient way possible. You'll learn everything you need to know to start using Evernote to its full potential straight away.

SAMPLE RESUME

Your Name
Your Address
Your Address
A professional-sounding email
Your Phone Number

SUMMARY   **Explain who you are and what type of job you are looking for in a single sentence.** You can bold the first part and leave the rest not bold, but always define yourself. Employers like simple definitions.

SKILLS   List your most relevant special skills, including anything you know how to do, anything you've previously accomplished, a general description of your familiarity with technology, etc. We'll list specific programs next.

APPLICATIONS   List specific computer programs, separated by commas, that you know how to use or that you have used previously. Loading this up front helps keyword searchers screen your resume and pick it.

WORK HISTORY

Year – Present   Employer Name – City, State *(https://website-of-employer)*

Your Job Title
In past tense, as if you don't work there anymore, describe what you were responsible for and what you accomplished. The top item will be your most recent job.

Year – Year   Employer Name – City, State *(https://website-of-employer)*

Your Job Title
In past tense, as if you don't work there anymore, describe what you were responsible for and what you accomplished. Use as many line items as you can reasonably fit. Remember, when possible, you want the resume to be one page.

Year – Year   Employer Name – City, State *(https://website-of-employer)*

Your Job Title
In past tense, as if you don't work there anymore, describe what you were responsible for and what you accomplished. If you've been in the job market for a long time, leave out your older, less relevant jobs unless they speak directly to what you're applying to.

Year – Year   Employer Name – City, State *(https://website-of-employer)*

Your Job Title
In past tense, as if you don't work there anymore, describe what you were responsible for and what you accomplished. For example, if you're running out of "real estate" on your resume, some of the first jobs you had out of school probably no longer matter to your degree.

If you have room, don't be afraid to do a second paragraph under each line item, or use bullet points. If you are just entering the job market, you won't have a lot of work history, so instead you'll focus on your academic credentials, clubs you were in, descriptions of your work ethic, etc. You can fit those in under the summary (by adding a new paragraph after your first single-sentence description) or place them in new paragraphs under Education and Credentials.

EDUCATION   **List any degrees you've earned in bold with the year you earned it,** then the school name/location. **Take as many line items as you have different degrees.**

CREDENTIALS   Here, list any special credentials or certifications you have.
Even if they're not relevant to the job, they say things about you.
If you're a martial arts instructor, you know CPR, whatever, put that here.

REFERENCES   Available on request. <-- *Always include this part, but don't bluff. Have the references ready if they ask you. Remember,. your goal for the resume is to get everything onto one page. Use this format and play with the spacing between line items if you need to. This basic structure is a very sound, reliable resume.*

TEXT-BASED RESUME

Your Name
Your Address
Your Address
A professional-sounding email
Your Phone Number

SUMMARY

Explain who you are and what type of job you are looking for in a single sentence. You can bold the first part and leave the rest not bold, but always define yourself. Employers like simple definitions.

SKILLS

List your most relevant special skills, including anything you know how to do, anything you've previously accomplished, a general description of your familiarity with technology, etc. We'll list specific programs next.

APPLICATIONS

List specific computer programs, separated by commas, that you know how to use or that you have used previously. Loading this up front helps keyword searchers screen your resume and pick it.

WORK HISTORY

Year – Present
Employer Name – City, State
(https://website-of-employer)

Your Job Title

In past tense, as if you don't work there anymore, describe what you were responsible for and what you accomplished. The top item will be your most recent job.

Year – Year
Employer Name – City, State
(https://website-of-employer)

Your Job Title

In past tense, as if you don't work there anymore, describe what you were responsible for and what you accomplished. Use as many line items as you can reasonably fit. Remember, when possible, you want the resume to be one page.

Year – Year
Employer Name – City, State
(https://website-of-employer)

Your Job Title

In past tense, as if you don't work there anymore, describe what you were responsible for and what you accomplished. If you've been in the job market for a long time, leave out your older, less relevant jobs unless they speak directly to what you're applying to.

Year – Year
Employer Name – City, State
(https://website-of-employer)

Your Job Title

In past tense, as if you don't work there anymore, describe what you were responsible for and what you accomplished. For example, if you're running out of "real estate" on your resume, some of the first jobs you had out of school probably no longer matter to your degree.

If you have room, don't be afraid to do a second paragraph under each line item, or use bullet points. If you are just entering the job market, you won't have a lot of work history, so instead you'll focus on your academic credentials, clubs you were in, descriptions of your work ethic, etc. You can fit those in under the summary (by adding a new paragraph after your first single-sentence description) or place them in new paragraphs under Education and Credentials.

EDUCATION

List any degrees you've earned in bold with the year you earned it, then the school name/location.

Take as many line items as you have different degrees.

CREDENTIALS

Here, list any special credentials or certifications you have.

Even if they're not relevant to the job, they say things about you.

If you're a martial arts instructor, you know CPR, whatever, put that here.

REFERENCES

Available on request. <-- Always include this part, but don't bluff. Have the references ready if they ask you. Remember,. your goal for the resume is to get everything onto one page. Use this format and play with the spacing between line items if you need to. This basic structure is a very sound, reliable resume.

KEYWORD RESUME

Business Analyst I - *[redacted]*

Description

Position Overview:

This client facing role of Business Analyst I is required in a fast paced team environment where we are managing multiple projects and client requirements on an ongoing basis. The successful candidate must be a strong creative and analytical thinker with strong documentation and planning skills and enjoy daily interaction with external clients.

Responsibilities:

    Design and implement simple solutions in order to solve complex business problems

    Gather and document business requirements

    Actively participate in project team meetings and lead when necessary

    Define, recommend and build opportunities to automate existing systems processes

    Participant at regular Client Support meetings

    Develop and produce documentation and testing material to support client initiatives/implementations

    Develop and implement new programs and services that cater to the client's unique needs and expectations

Qualifications

Required Knowledge:

    Knowledge of claim adjudication principals; Pharmacy Benefit Management is an asset

    Proven ability to collect requirements and document business processes and client requirements

    Excellent interpersonal and communications skills

    Experience analysing and reporting on performance and utilisation data

Required Skills & Abilities:

    Strong written and verbal communication skills

    Highly developed personal planning and organisational skills

    Demonstrated ability to adapt quickly to change

    Ability to work in a fast paced environment while adhering to service level commitments

    Strong analytical problem identification, and problem solving skills

    Strong customer focus

    Capable and willing learner who proactively researches solutions to business challenges

    Highly proficient in Excel, Visio, MS Access

    Required Professional Designation/Certification

    University Degree or related College Diploma in Health Science, Computer Science or Business/Commerce

Required Experience:

mentioned twice!

Add tag

PROFESSIONAL COVER LETTER EXAMPLE

Today's Date

Address of Employer
Address of Employer
Address of Employer

Dear Human Resources Manager,

I'm writing in response to your job listing for [position]. I believe I am ideally suited to this position, based on [your reasons for being a good fit, including your experience and skills]. I have attached my resume for your consideration and would welcome the opportunity to discuss the position with you at your convenience.

Kind Regards,

Your Name
(with your signature above; you can scan or photograph your signature and insert it into these documents if you're feeling fancy)

JOYCE FEUSTEL'S LINKEDIN PROFILE

Joyce Feustel helps people, especially those age 50 and up, to become more effective using social media, especially LinkedIn and Facebook.

She works with business owners, business development professionals, business consultants, job seekers, and more—ranging from entrepreneurs to people in large corporations.

Find her at www.boomerssocialmediatutor.com.

Contact

720-984-1162 (Work)
joyce@boomerssocialmediatut
or.com

www.linkedin.com/in/
joycefeustelsocialmediatrainer
(LinkedIn)
boomerssocialmediatutor.com
(Other)
www.meetup.com/meetup-group-
simplify-your-social-media/ (Other)
www.facebook.com/
boomerssocialmediatutor/ (Other)

Top Skills

LinkedIn Training

Social Media Marketing

Entrepreneurship

Languages

English (Native or Bilingual)

Certifications

Online Marketing & Social Media
Certification

Honors-Awards

District 26 Toastmaster of the Year

Distinguished Toastmaster

Top Graduate: University of
Wisconsin - Madison

Publications

Use LinkedIn to Enhance Business
Relationships

Heart of a Toastmaster

Seek Your Peak to Find Your Spark

Three Best Practices for Using
LinkedIn

Virtual Visit from Taiwan

Joyce Feustel

LinkedIn Coach & Trainer | Speaker & Presenter | Baby Boomer
Specialist | Business Owners | Job Seekers | Making Social Media
Simple, Easy & Fun
Denver Metropolitan Area

Summary

Does LinkedIn mystify you? Have you ever wondered what folks
mean when they say "optimize your LinkedIn profile?"

Do your posts on LinkedIn get attention from the people you want to
reach?

If you've ever asked yourself these questions, and especially if you
are born between 1946 and 1964, I can help you. Being on the older
end of the baby boomer generation, I identify with the frustrations
that folks in my age group have with LinkedIn and social media in
general.

My clients are primarily baby boomers who have their own business
or are job seekers. I help them to be more effective and productive
on LinkedIn and Facebook.

Typically, my clients and I meet virtually (although I occasionally
meet local clients in person) using Zoom or another
videoconferencing site. We start with a detailed review of their
LinkedIn profile or Facebook business page.

Many changes can easily be made by my clients in real time, with
a few items requiring some homework on their part. In addition,
we systemically review LinkedIn's or Facebook's settings and their
functions. Then, I help them to streamline the time they spend
posting, searching and engaging with others.

You might wonder how someone my age became a social media
tutor, trainer and coach. Here's how it happened – back in 2010,
when I was 61 years old, the company where I worked added social
media to its marketing mix. Folks on the sales team, including me,

were asked to encourage our current and potential clients to engage with our social media.

My manager told me that I did the best job of anyone on our team of getting our current and potential clients to engage with our company's social media. He encouraged me to help other baby boomers learn how to use their social media. I launched my business that fall and went full-time in 2013, when I retired from a 17-year career in sales.

Testimonials from clients:

"What a find - Joyce is just what I need right now. I am using her services to help me better understand LinkedIn. I find her coaching refreshing. She is very knowledgeable, and she is patient with my pace.'"
Janice Hurley - Owner of Janice Hurley: The Image Expert

"My company does sales training and workshops. We needed some online marketing help using LinkedIn to promote our company. Joyce quickly sized up our situation. She clearly and effectively showed us exactly where we could improve."
Roger Kleckner, President, Ascent Sales Advisors

Contact me to become more effective in your use of LinkedIn and Facebook - joyce@boomerssocialmediatutor.com

Experience

Boomers' Social Media Tutor
10 years 10 months

LinkedIn Trainer | Corporate LinkedIn Consultant | LinkedIn Webinars & Workshops
June 2013 - Present (8 years 2 months)
Denver Metropolitan Area

I offer LinkedIn training, presentations, workshops, and webinars in a wide variety of settings - both virtual and face-to-face.

Groups I work with include:

• Professional and trade organizations
• Business networking and membership organizations
• Job seeker groups
• Teams within a company, such as a team of commercial realtors
• Network marketing teams

Typically, I share tips on how to optimize a LinkedIn profile, and how to effectively search, share information and engage with others on LinkedIn.

Trainings vary from as short as 30 minutes to as long as two hours and are tailored to meet the needs of the participants. The training package includes short individual tutoring sessions for attendees who need additional help.

In addition, I share LinkedIn tips and trends as a guest on a wide range of podcasts, from those that focus on personal and professional growth to those with a more business-centric approach.

Learn more about my LinkedIn training and speaking by contacting me at joyce@boomerssocialmediatutor.com or going to my website at www.boomerssocialmediatutor.com.

Testimonials

"Joyce is a stellar human being and is truly dedicated towards helping boomers learn how to navigate LinkedIn successfully. It was such an honor to interview her on my podcast. She is articulate and knowledgeable, and she genuinely seeks to offer value at every opportunity."
Marisa Huston, Podcaster at Live Blissed Out

"We recently did a training at my company RE | Solutions and everyone walked away more knowledgeable and armed with tools to improve their experience going forward. We are looking forward to becoming dynamic users of LinkedIn."
Claire Skougor, RE | Solutions

Founder | Social Media Trainer & Tutor | Social Media Consultant
October 2010 - Present (10 years 10 months)
Denver Metropolitan Area

I provide personalized coaching, tutoring and consulting to help business owners and job seekers to more effectively and productively use such social media sites as LinkedIn and Facebook.

My clients include business owners, coaches, corporate professionals, job seekers and more. Although I primarily serve people 55 and older, I work with people of all ages.

We start with a detailed review of their LinkedIn profile or Facebook business page. Many changes can easily be made by my client in real time, with a few items requiring some "homework" on their part. I guide my clients in how they can update their LinkedIn profile themselves or their Facebook business page.

In addition, we systemically review LinkedIn's or Facebook's settings and their functions. Then, I help them to streamline the time they spend posting, searching and engaging with others.

Upon request, I can make changes to a LinkedIn profile on behalf of a client. Clients must already have had a one-hour tutoring session with me to be eligible for this service.

Learn more about my individual coaching, tutoring, consulting by contacting me at joyce@boomerssocialmediatutor.com or going to my website at www.boomerssocialmediatutor.com.

Testimonials:

"I just spent an hour with Joyce Feustel of Boomers' Social Media Tutor to tighten up my LinkedIn profile. The best hour I've ever spent. Joyce knows what she's talking about, and does an excellent job conveying it. Have questions or need help with your profile, call Joyce."

Dan Light, Dan Light Consulting | Accomplished Entrepreneur | Early-Stage Business Advocate

"Joyce conducted a comprehensive interview of me, synthesized what I shared, and then went into LinkedIn and updated my profile. Since the process went so seamlessly, I asked her to do the same thing for my business partner and husband Peter. Again, she did a great job."
Camilla Manly, Akamai Systems Consulting

No Limit Over 50

Social Media Professional Speaker and Presenter
2013 - Present (8 years)
Denver Metropolitan Area

I offer webinars, keynotes, conference breakout sessions, and presentations - primarily on LinkedIn. Some representative events:

• "Showcase Yourself and Network on LinkedIn" a webinar for the Material Handling Equipment Distributors Association (MHEDA).

• "LinkedIn as a Marketing and Networking Tool," a keynote for Women in Business, a program of the South Metro Denver Chamber of Commerce.

• "Ways for Nonprofit Leaders to Leverage LinkedIn," a three-part online lunch and learn series co-sponsored by nonprofit consultant Julianna Nelson, Founder of Phillinnova and myself.

• "Ways to Search on LinkedIn to Find More Clients," a presentation for TiE Denver.

• "Leverage LinkedIn to Land Your Next Job," a training at the Job Search Skills Camp held by the Mile Hi Chapter of the Project Management Institute.

• "Attract More Clients with LinkedIn," a breakout session at the Annual Conference of the National Organization of Trusted Advisors.

• "Use LinkedIn to Enhance Your Face to Face Networking," a presentation for the Association for Talent Development – Rocky Mountain Chapter.

Looking for a dynamic speaker or trainer for your association or organization's next event? Email joyce@boomerssocialmediatutor.com

Testimonials:

"Thank you so much, Joyce! You did a great job and added so much value for our members!!! I definitely think you should think about stand-up comedy! Perhaps 'America's Got Talent?!' You are a genuine, smart and giving person." AnnaMarie Kendall, Marketing Communication Manager, Material Handling Equipment Distributors Association (MHEDA)

Bob Poole & Steve Dotto

"Joyce is an expert at LinkedIn and an excellent professional speaker. Joyce presented to the SHE Leads Group, and she was engaging, organized, and very knowledgeable. She checked throughout the presentation for questions and answered all our questions. I highly recommend Joyce if you are looking for LinkedIn training or a presenter for your group or organization."
Beth Boen, Founder of SHE Leads Group

Founder | Organizer | Social Media Instructor & Discussion Facilitator
December 2017 - Present (3 years 8 months)
Denver Metropolitan Area

I host this Meetup group that meets on the 2nd Tuesdays of each month from 1:30 - 3: p.m. via Zoom. Meetings are free to attend, and RSVPs are required through Meetup.

This Meetup group is for people who are not professionals in the field of social media AND who are business owners or business professionals who would say Yes to any one or more of these questions:

• Do you want to learn more about social media in a low-key safe setting?
• Do your competitors have a stronger social media presence than you do?
• Do you get frustrated when people tease you for not being "social media savvy?"
• Do you dread using social media?
• Do you like to help others use social media more effectively?

Get more information and join the Meetup group at:

https://www.meetup.com/meetup-group-simplify-your-social-media/

Testimonials from attendees:

"Thank you, Joyce! I continue to learn so much from the Simplify Your Social Media Meetup Group. Every event has presented a treasure trove of information and solid connections for business owners, entrepreneurs, and anyone seeking to augment her/his online presence."
Patricia Moore, Writer, Photographer, Book Designer, Owner of Time Travelers: Everyone Has a Story

"I'm grateful for all I'm learning as a member of Joyce Feustel's Simplify Your Social Media Meetup Group. We benefit not only from Joyce's expertise but also from the valuable ideas shared by our fellow members."
Jan Stapleman, Writer - Fearless Communications

"That was one of the best Zooms I've been on since the pandemic began. I'm excited to 'meetup' with this group again. They were pretty darned fabulous."
Patricia Finley, Artist

Strategic Trusted Advisors Roundtable
Board Member
January 2019 - Present (2 years 7 months)
Denver Metropolitan Area

STAR-Denver is a connecting group for professionals who serve in a trusted advisor capacity and have been in their industry for at least seven years.

I currently serve as program chair and previously served as board member at large and as chair of the membership committee

Colorado Free University
LinkedIn Instructor & Course Creator
September 2013 - Present (7 years 11 months)
Denver Metropolitan Area

Colorado Free University (CFU) is a lifelong learning center based in Denver, Colorado, that offers a wide array of skill-based and enrichment courses. More of a learning network than a traditional school, CFU draws its teachers from the community, and all teachers are independent contractors.

I teach the "Use LinkedIn to Grow Your Business" class either through Zoom or at Colorado Free University, 7653 E. 1st Place, Denver 80230. Go to www.freeu.com for a complete list of classes. The class is offered as a three-hour, one-time session.

Testimonial from one of my CFU students:

"Joyce breaks down the features of LinkedIn in a very understandable manner. I was impressed by her knowledge of the platform and her friendly presentation style. I highly recommend her."

Caitlin Berve

Bob Poole & Steve Dotto

Editor and Owner, Ignited Ink Writing
Instructor, Colorado Free University

Toastmasters International
District 26 Social Media Chair
August 2011 - June 2013 (1 year 11 months)
Denver Metropolitan Area

Toastmasters International is a world leader in communication and leadership development. District 26 serves over 3,000 members and over 180 clubs in Colorado, Wyoming and western Nebraska.

I coordinated the district's social media team - which consists of Toastmasters with expertise in Facebook, LinkedIn, and Twitter. This team uses the district's social media sites to post announcements of contests, conferences, leadership training opportunities and other activities sponsored by District 26 Toastmasters.

College for Financial Planning
Enrollment Advisor
August 2006 - March 2013 (6 years 8 months)
Denver Metropolitan Area

• Assessed which educational programs provided by the college best meet the needs of the professionals in the financial services industry and guide them in their decision-making process.
• Enrolled people in the financial planning and financial services industry (and those who wanted to enter this field) in the appropriate professional educational programs.
• Provided ongoing direction to students enrolled in the college's professional education programs.

Toastmasters International
District 26 Club Coaching Chair
July 2007 - December 2009 (2 years 6 months)
Denver Metropolitan Area

Toastmasters International is a world leader in communication and leadership development. District 26 serves over 3,000 members and over 180 clubs in Colorado, Wyoming and western Nebraska.

• Identified Toastmasters Clubs in the district with 12 or fewer members who wanted assistance of a club coach from another Toastmasters Club.

• Recruited club coaches and matched them with coach-eligible clubs - oversaw these matches and provided support to club coaches as needed.
• A high percentage of these clubs achieved their club goals during my tenure, and the district was the level of distinguished, and achieved its goals as well.

University of Phoenix
Associate Enrollment Counselor
March 2004 - August 2006 (2 years 6 months)
Denver Metropolitan Area

The University of Phoenix offers a wide range of undergraduate and graduate degree programs.

• Enrolled students in bachelor's and master's degree programs offered by the University of Phoenix
• Set appointments for enrollment counselors to meet with prospective students
• Consistently had a high ratio of students showing up for these appointments and then enrolling into the appropriate educational program

Toastmasters International
District 26 Governor
July 2005 - June 2006 (1 year)
Denver Metropolitan Area

Toastmasters International is a world leader in communication and leadership development. District 26 serves over 3,000 members and over 180 clubs in Colorado, Wyoming and western Nebraska.

Directed activities of 50 volunteer leaders.

Better Business Bureau serving Greater Denver and Central Colorado
Membership Representative
October 2000 - May 2003 (2 years 8 months)
Denver Metropolitan Area

• Met with business owners to help them determine if joining the BBB would benefit their business and if so, processed membership payment.
• Top producer in new member sales in 2002.

Education

Bob Poole & Steve Dotto

University of Wisconsin-Madison
M.A. School of Business and Department of Preventive Medicine, Health Services Administration

University of Wisconsin-Madison
M.S. Curriculum and Instruction, Health Education

University of Wisconsin-Madison
B.S. School of Education, English/Language Arts Teacher Education

University of Phoenix-Colorado Campus
Business Management

ACKNOWLEDGMENTS

This book has its own story to tell. It is the story of how an idea became a possibility and then became a reality. It's the story of how two people who have never met in person became friends across country borders and with the help of a generous and talented team of people spent much of 2021 working to create a guide for our fellow Gen Xer and Boomer family. We want to acknowledge and thank them.

For their creative and professional editing assistance, Phil Elmore, Bryna Kranzler, and Judith Guertin made our words sing, fixed our errors, and gently prodded us to do better.

We had a team of generous and creative volunteer beta readers from the Grey Wave community read one of the last iterations of the manuscript and offer invaluable advice. They are David Earl, David Gouthro, Francisca de Zwager, Gary Drouillard, Janice Sanders, Judith Guertin, Mary Jo Barnes, and Peter Blok.

Jana Rade, owner of Impact Studios in Ontario, is a fantastic graphic artist. She designed the cover and other elements as part of our marketing campaign.

Liz Azyan, a London-based graphic designer and a member of the Grey Wave team, created our video trailer, website, and additional consulting ideas.

April Heavens-Woodcock is the Grey Wave community manager and was indispensable in her support of all of us.

Joann Poole provided proofreading services. Her ability to find misspelled words and grammatical errors after everything looks perfect always amazes Bob.

Joyce Feustal, the founder of Boomers' Social Media Tutor, taught us about LinkedIn for our generation and provided tips and her personal LinkedIn profile.

Last but not least, we thank Rick Lite and the team at Stress Free Book Marketing for their professional services in putting the final touches on the book and getting it to our publisher.

ABOUT THE AUTHORS

Bob Poole

With over 45 years of business experience as an entrepreneur helping other companies grow through creative consulting solutions, Bob has solved problems and created opportunities for as many types of businesses as you can imagine.

During the Vietnam War, Bob served in the US Navy. During part of his naval service, he was stationed onboard the USS Recovery (ARS 43), a rescue and salvage ship. Bob became one of a few enlisted personnel in the US Navy to earn and be assigned as Underway Officer of The Deck.

As a photojournalist and professional photographer during the late '60s and early '70s, his peers and clients recognized Bob as an outstanding talent, leading to a national photography achievement award from Eastman Kodak. In addition, his fellows in Professional Photographers of America consistently acknowledged him for his outstanding work.

A talent for creating marketing campaigns led to him becoming more involved in sales and marketing. His first position with a company other than his own was in sales for 3M Company. In 1980, he was recognized by 3M and awarded their highest sales honor and was their guest at the 1980 Winter Olympics in Lake Placid.

With a desire to share his passion for business with others, he has conducted over 150 sales, marketing, and technology seminars and workshops for a wide variety of companies, associations, and individuals in the United States, Europe, Canada, Australia, and Asia. In addition, as a member of the National Speakers Association, he was one of the International Center for Professional Speaking founders in Tempe, AZ. He has enjoyed traveling for business and pleasure to over 35 countries and six continents.

Companies and individuals use his sales consulting program, "Listen First – Sell Later"®, to implement a highly successful approach to selling both products and services. He is the author of three previous books, and his work has also appeared in many newspapers, magazines, and trade journals. In addition, his website https://bob-poole.com/ has a combination of almost 1,000 free blog posts and podcast episodes. At 72 years old, he is creating follow-up products and services to enhance the Listen First – Sell Later sales program. He firmly believes that "age is a state of mind."

Steve Dotto

Steve Dotto is Canada's favorite geek. For over 20 years, as host and executive producer of Dotto Tech, a nationally syndicated TV show, Steve entertained and educated millions of Canadians on all aspects of technology.

After spending 20 years in traditional broadcast, Steve re-invented himself, learning the world of social media, online community building, and Internet Marketing as he built his YouTube channel into his new career.

His passion is teaching Baby Boomers and Gen Xers how to remain relevant in the digital age, how we can re-invent ourselves and grow side hustles into successful online businesses.

He has a gift for making complex concepts easy to understand. Steve takes the world of technology and makes it relevant in your life.

A background in theatre and comedy, including a short stint with the famed comedy troupe, Second City, provides for a unique and often humorous perspective on the works of technology.

YouTube is Steve's new network of choice. He serves two communities, a traditional "How To and Productivity" stream, which follows his TV tradition, and a new focus on learning the keys to growing and ultimately monetizing a Social Network, specifically, a YouTube channel.